RENTS

'What you would never guess about *Rents* in advance is that it is so funny. Here we are, faced with a story about youthful prostitution (male), poverty and urban paranoia . . . And yet, there it is at the Lyric Studio, Hammersmith, rolling them in the aisles. *Rents* is a play which touches on all kinds of problems, but it is not by any means a problem play . . . And, thank heavens, it is a gay play only in the sense that all the principals are gay men, not at all in the sense that it is about The Problem . . . A wholly enjoyable experience . . . Michael Wilcox is unmistakably a born dramatist.'

John Russell Taylor, *Plays and Players*

Rents was first seen at the Traverse Theatre, Edinburgh, in 1979 and revived at the Lyric Studio, Hammersmith, in 1982. This edition contains the *Rents* Guide to Edinburgh and the *Rents* Appendix containing some of the earlier drafts of the play in which subsequently discarded characters make their appearance.

The front cover design is from the original Traverse production and is by Adrian Mudd.

in the same series

SAMBA
by Michael Abbensetts
EAST-WEST & IS UNCLE JACK A CONFORMIST?
by Andrey Amalrik
SORE THROATS & SONNETS OF LOVE AND OPPOSITION
by Howard Brenton
THIRTEENTH NIGHT & A SHORT SHARP SHOCK!
by Howard Brenton (*A Short Sharp Shock!* written with Tony Howard)
POOR TOM & TINA
by David Cregan
TEENDREAMS
WRECKERS
by David Edgar
THE HOUSE
by David Halliwell
BASTARD ANGEL
FROZEN ASSETS
SUS
by Barrie Keeffe
SERGEANT OLA AND HIS FOLLOWERS
by David Lan
LAVENDER BLUE & NOLI ME TANGERE
by John Mackendrick
AMERICAN BUFFALO, SEXUAL PERVERSITY IN CHICAGO & DUCK VARIATIONS
by David Mamet
THICK AS THIEVES
by Tony Marchant
NICE, RUM AN' COCA COLA & WELCOME HOME JACKO
PLAY MAS, INDEPENDENCE & MEETINGS
by Mustapha Matura
LUNATIC AND LOVER
by Michael Meyer
AMERICAN DAYS
FAVOURITE NIGHTS & CAUGHT ON A TRAIN
SHOUT ACROSS THE RIVER
STRAWBERRY FIELDS
THE SUMMER PARTY
by Stephen Poliakoff
BRIMSTONE AND TREACLE
by Dennis Potter
GOOD
by C. P. Taylor
THE ACCRINGTON PALS
by Peter Whelan
SUGAR AND SPICE & TRIAL RUN
W.C.P.C.
by Nigel Williams
HAS 'WASHINGTON' LEGS & DINGO
BY Charles Wood

RENTS

MICHAEL WILCOX

A Methuen New Theatrescript
Methuen · London

A METHUEN PAPERBACK

First published as a paperback original in 1983 by Methuen London Ltd,
11 New Fetter Lane, London EC4P 4EE

Printed by Expression Printers Ltd, London N7

ISBN 0 413 51810 8

Rents was first produced, in this five actor version, by the Traverse Theatre Company during the 1979 Edinburgh International Festival. The cast was as follows:

PHIL MACFERSON	David Bannerman
ROBERT	Jimmy Chisholm
RICHARD RIDLEY	David Whitaker
EDDIE	Campbell Morrison
ALBERT *the accountant* PETER *the solicitor* SPIDER THOMAS *from Harpenden* MR MACFERSON	Carey Wilson

Directed by Chris Parr
Designed by Adrian Mudd
Lighting by Dave Horn
Sound by Matt McKenzie

The action is set in Edinburgh, Scotland, in the mid-1970's.

For the revival at the Lyric Studio, Hammersmith, from 17 April to 8 May 1982. RICHARD RIDLEY was played by Jonathon Newth.

The 'Rents' Guide to Edinburgh

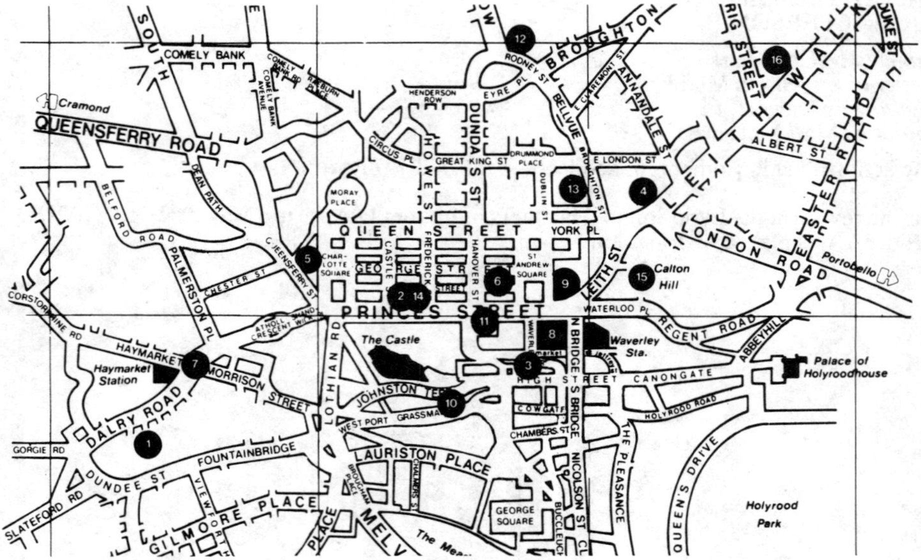

1. Phil's Flat
2. The Kenilworth (The K)
3. Robert's Shop
4. Dragon Pearl
5. Edinburgh Film Theatre
6. The Golden Egg
7. Haymarket - Phil meets Peter the solicitor
8. North British Hotel
9. GHQ
10. The Traverse
11. National Gallery - Phil meets Spider
12. Loon Fung
13. S.M.G. (Scottish Minorities' Group) Office
14. Crawfords
15. Calton Hill - Robert meets Spider
16. Mop and Bucket's flat in Leith

ACT ONE

PHIL *at his apartment off the Dalry Road.*

PHIL: I need a man . . . a real man. Oh Scotland . . . where has your virility trickled? What I want is a worker, hot from the production line . . . with a day's sweat on him. Body odours really excite me . . . saltiness mingled with fragrant machine oil. I need a Scot bright-eyed from an oil rig . . . a boiler maker . . . a crofter from the Outer Hebrides. The best I've done this week was Malcolm from the Golden Wonder factory.

ROBERT *at the apartment.*

ROBERT: I came on the scene when I was fifteen, travelling in to Edinburgh from Livingstone at weekends. I was astonished at the sort of custom I had . . . all these men coming all over me in the most unlikely situations. If a guy took me to the cinema I'd let him screw me in the bog while the other kids were queuing for ice creams. I couldn't stop myself. I just loved to see a grown man get that excited about me . . . my body . . . God . . . my body . . . and feeling the tension . . . and sweat of him when he came . . . and his dejection as he cleaned himself up afterwards. One guy punched me in the mouth when I laughed at him. I went with him again . . .

EDDIE *on the streets of Edinburgh.*

EDDIE: I first met Phil MacFerson in Rose Street . . . just along from the Kenilworth. This was a couple of years ago. He just came up to me from nowhere and started talking. I can't remember what he said . . . but we ended up going for a drink. And only after about half an hour did we realise that it was his mother that was going with my Norma! Well . . . she was mine. I mean . . . we were together and getting by. It wasn't all . . . oh . . . never mind. But not content with one half of his bloody family taking off with my Norma, here's this bent bastard chatting me up . . . *me*! I never realised what he was after . . . not at first. He never said anything . . . but it just dawned on me . . . slowly. I never went with him. *I didn't.*

RICHARD *is preparing to leave his house in Newcastle 130 miles south of Edinburgh, across the border in England. The record that is playing is the 2nd movement of Mozart's Devertimento KV 138 (The Italian Quartet Philips 6599 663).*

RICHARD: I've been up since half past five. It's been one of those special mornings when the sun wakes you up and you really don't want to stay in bed a second longer. I was tempted to do some work in the garden, but drank a pot of tea instead.

Music sounds so good this morning. This is part of a Mozart Divertimento played by the Italian Quartet . . .

No one in their right mind would leave home on a day like this. I've got to stand in for this lecturer at Charles Stuart College up in Edinburgh. Just for a few weeks. It's extra cash, I suppose. Makes a change from Newcastle Poly . . . There isn't a decent record shop in Edinburgh. They sell everything at full price, even the boxed sets. If you're going to buy something, you might as well pay as little as possible. Edinburgh's a full price city.

The flat of PHIL *and* ROBERT *in Edinburgh, off the Dalry Road. It's just after eight o'clock in the morning.* ROBERT *has dashed across the road to the supermarket, that opens at eight, to fetch provisions. He arrives back a few minutes later.*

PHIL: Success?

ROBERT: Of course!

ROBERT *puts down a carrier bag with a few groceries in it.* PHIL *looks through it, unimpressed.*

PHIL: Tea and a packet of biscuits!

ROBERT: You've got to pay for something.

ROBERT *has various articles hidden all over him after his shop-lifting raid. He produces them one by one, and throws them across to* PHIL.

Coffee . . . beans . . . steak and kidney pies . . . three! Beans . . . salad cream . . . beans . . . whiskers

PHIL: We haven't got a cat!

ROBERT: Don't be fussy! Beans . . . tin of carrots . . . mushy peas . . . beans . . . a kit-kat . . .

PHIL: Only one?

ROBERT: Beans . . .

PHIL: We've got over 200 cans of beans in the cupboard. Can you not resist pinching beans for a month or two?

ROBERT: They're on special offer this week.

PHIL: What's wrong with sardines?

ROBERT: Hold on! Sardines . . . sardines . . . sardines . . . and sardines . . . and beans . . .

PHIL: Terrific!

ROBERT: Aren't you pleased?

PHIL: What am I doing in college, Robert?

ROBERT: What am I doing in a run-down men's shop? The new jeans are in.

PHIL: I want a pair.

ROBERT: Which side are you hanging this season?

PHIL: I haven't got any money.

ROBERT: Stand up . . . prominent leftist . . .

PHIL: Are you selling tailored jeans?

ROBERT: No . . . but every time a man comes into the shop I reach for my tape measure. I'm Edinburgh's leading authority on inside legs.

PHIL: I'm 30-31 . . . I want a pair.

ROBERT: Why do you always plead like a little child when you want something? Stop pleading.

PHIL: We'll nick 'em . . . this morning.

ROBERT: No way.

PHIL: Yes.

ROBERT: She watches me like a hawk . . . no.

PHIL: Yes.

ROBERT: How?

PHIL: Put two pairs of jeans – size 30-31 . . . onto one coat hanger . . . right? Then I'll come in with a bag . . . some other shopping . . . don't recognise me . . . you mustn't recognise me . . .

ROBERT: I said no . . .

PHIL: . . . and then come and measure me . . . no, serve me!

ROBERT: I'm not going to.

PHIL: . . . give me the hanger with the two jeans on . . . I'll try them on . . .

ROBERT: We have stalls with swing doors . . . like a Western saloon . . .

PHIL: I'll put one pair in my bag . . . and try on the other pair . . .

ROBERT: They can see everything . . .

PHIL: . . . then I'll decide not to buy . . . and give the jeans back . . . and away . . . done it . . . we've done it! The perfect crime . . . true genius for you.

ROBERT: What do I do with the empty coat hanger?

PHIL: Easy . . . lose it . . .

ROBERT: Lose it . . .

PHIL: Yes.

ROBERT: I'll shit myself.

PHIL: You won't.

ROBERT: I will.

PHIL: You hate her . . . think how much you hate her, Robert . . . how much does she pay you an hour?

ROBERT: I don't know.

PHIL: How much?

ROBERT: About 60 pence.

PHIL: Robbery! She's making a fortune out of you. How can you rent yourself out for 60 pence an hour? Is that all you're worth? That bitch has corrupted your sense of values. She's ripped you off so much she owes us jeans . . . cords . . . Wrangler shirts . . . Oh Robert . . . we must do this thing together.

ROBERT: I'll see.

PHIL: I'll be in at ten o'clock precisely.

ROBERT: What do I get out of it?

RICHARD *at college.*

RICHARD: Now I've just been told . . . twenty minutes ago . . . that I'm going to be lecturing you on the following plays. Everyman in the edition by A. C. Cawley

. . . *Henry IV Part One* . . . and just to confuse you totally . . . *Henry IV* by Pirandello . . . We'll be using Eric Bentley's edition. There's a set of those in the bookroom. The Everymans are being used by another group and photocopies will be available later in the week.

Now . . . you may be wondering . . . as I am . . . what these three plays have in common . . . why they've been lumped together. Unlikely bedfellows . . .

(*Aside*:) The buggers at this place don't waste much time. I'm shoved in to lecture on Everyman at half an hour's notice. Thank God the students haven't read it either . . .

So the Messenger tells the audience right at the start that life is *transitory* . . . we're just passing through life and that judgement awaits us. Nothing lasts. And that *that* knowledge should guide our moral conduct. Now I'd like you to consider . . . er . . . well . . . if you don't believe in God . . . or at least . . . in Divine Judgement . . . whether the purpose of Everyman . . . which the messenger points out to us . . . has any moral force. We may believe that at our death, the light is just switched out forever . . . and that's that. And if our conduct during life is not to be regulated by fear of what might come to us after death, why not just live for the excitement . . . the passion . . . the fleshliness . . . of life . . . and to hell with repressive, false morality?

(*Aside*:) They seem to believe every word I say! Half the girls are scribbling away as though I've just stepped down from Mount Parnassus.

RICHARD *sees a face pressed up against the window in the door. It's* PHIL.

In the middle of my lecture a face is pressed against the window in the door . . . staring . . . like a challenge. There he is again, lurking by the toilets . . .

PHIL: Richard . . .

RICHARD: What? Oh . . .

PHIL: Are you going for lunch?

RICHARD: Where is it? I'm lost in this place.

PHIL: Take these . . . I'll show you.

PHIL *hands him luncheon vouchers.*

RICHARD: Oh . . .

PHIL: Lunch vouchers . . . just hand them over to the woman at the till . . . lunches aren't bad. I've got plenty . . . don't worry . . . Do you play pool?

RICHARD: Yes.

PHIL: We'll have a game after lunch. You're from Newcastle.

RICHARD: Aye . . .

PHIL: I was down there a few weeks ago . . . at the Casablanca . . .

RICHARD: You naughty boy.

PHIL: Will you come to a film tonight? I want you to come, Richard . . . come and see *Fox* with me . . . you must come and see it with me. I don't want to go alone . . . none of my friends . . . none of them will come . . . I don't want to go alone . . . I want you to come with me. I want to talk to you Richard . . . Richard I think you're someone I can talk to . . . I'm going home after lunch . . . we could meet . . .

RICHARD: What's your name again?

PHIL: Phil . . . just call me Phil . . . I don't like Philip . . . you needn't pay me in or anything . . . I'll pay for us both if you want . . . come with me to see *Fox* . . .

RICHARD: Let's go and have some lunch.

PHIL: Will you help me, Richard? I'm doing Vladimir for my assessment. The first seven pages of *Waiting for Godot*. I don't understand it. Will you help me Richard?

RICHARD: I'm hungry.

PHIL: It's this way. Do you like my new jeans?

They go.

ROBERT *is working in the men's shop.* EDDIE *enters.*

ROBERT: Look at the state of that!

EDDIE: What's your name?

ROBERT: What?

EDDIE: Why are you staring at me?

ROBERT: What?

EDDIE: Why do you keep staring down below my waist?

ROBERT: I'm not staring at you.

EDDIE: Are you trying to start an argument?

ROBERT: No. Do you want anything?

EDDIE: I'd love to suck you off.

ROBERT: Ahhh . . . get out of this shop . . . I'll call the police . . .

EDDIE: Do you sell studded belts?

ROBERT: No we don't . . . now please leave at once.

EDDIE: You're looking at me as though I was a poof or something . . .

ROBERT: I was not.

EDDIE: I know how to deal with queers.

ROBERT: Out!

EDDIE: I'll follow you home. I know you live with Phil MacFerson.

ROBERT: Jesus Christ . . .

EDDIE: See you around . . .

EDDIE *leaves.*

RICHARD *back at the college.*

RICHARD: . . . so I've agreed to meet Phil outside the cinema at 7.15 this evening. I didn't tell him I'd already seen *Fox* as part of a Fassbinder season at the Tyneside Film Theatre. I didn't like the film much anyway . . . two hours of homosexual misery. Who wants to pay money for that sort of shit? But I do want to watch Phil watching it . . . and I am on some sort of holiday. But now I'm going to take a trip round the record shops.

EDDIE *is following* ROBERT *after work.*

EDDIE: . . . you see Edinburgh's falling apart and I don't want to fall apart with it. Someone's got to make a stand and I'm not frightened of turning over a few stones. Your hands are bound to get dirty in a place like this. MacFerson's dirt. He has this habit of turning up and worming his way into people's lives. You know . . . like assaulting your life . . . indecently. And that bastard is free to walk around the streets. I've been out getting a new job today. Plenty of jobs in Edinburgh. There is no unemployment problem in this city. I could have got a job weeding in the botanical gardens . . . turned it down . . . took a job as a chef in The Golden Egg. I wanted a job with a uniform.

Back at PHIL*'s apartment,* PHIL *is with* ALBERT, *an accountant.*

PHIL: Have a coffee before you go, Albert?

ALBERT: No thanks, dear boy . . . I don't drink much coffee these days. It's partly the caffeine . . . keeps me awake . . . even in the afternoon. Gives me indigestion too . . . ulcers . . . always been a bit of a problem. Do you suffer?

PHIL: Not yet.

ALBERT: No. Too young. I blame them on calculators actually. Dreadful things. Have you got one?

PHIL: No.

ALBERT: Ohhh . . . I'll give you one for Christmas. I've always had a good head for figures . . . which . . . you will agree . . . is a help in my profession. I was slow and steady and got there in the end . . . as with other things, dear boy. Now I'm being left behind . . . my old mind you see. I like old fashioned things . . . Earl Gray Tea, Sir Walter Scott, Vaseline. Marmite is still delicious.

PHIL: I've never tried Marmite.

ALBERT: . . . on toast . . . for breakfast . . . and kippers. I love a good kipper. You must have breakfast with me sometime.

PHIL: Oh . . .

ALBERT: . . . and if you can spare time from your studies, perhaps you'll travel over to Glasgow with me for the opera. Janet Baker's singing Dorabella in *Cosi Fan Tutte.* It should be divine.

PHIL: I'm busy at the moment . . . practical assessments this term and finals next. I've got a few holes in my course work file to be plugged. Maybe later in the summer, Albert.

ALBERT: I'll take you out to dinner . . . make a real evening of it. Well . . . I'll be going. When shall I see you?

PHIL: I'm keeping myself to myself just now. I want to do well at college.

ALBERT: Very sensible. I haven't seen

you at Scottish Minorities Group meetings recently.

PHIL: No . . . it's all this reading I'm doing. I've no time.

ALBERT: Goodbye then. (*He leaves two £5 notes by the bed.*)

PHIL: See you Albert.

ALBERT: No doubt . . . no doubt. (*He leaves.*)

PHIL: My father drives long distance lorries. I've got a whole brood of half-brothers and sisters scattered around the borders and beyond. I think my father carries the brotherhood of man too far. Some of it has rubbed off onto me. We meet . . . always by accident . . . sometimes when I'm out shopping there's this tremendous hooting and there's father driving past waving at me . . . a big smile across his face. He rarely stops to talk. I suppose he treats all his progeny in the same manner. He's not on the phone and I can't keep track of the number of firms he works for. If I want to see him, I have to travel out to Wester Hailes on the off chance of him actually being there. He's a freelance like me.

ROBERT *bursts in.*

ROBERT: Phil . . . oh . . . Phil . . . I've been molested.

PHIL: That's great news, Robert . . . I'm happy for you.

ROBERT: No . . . no . . .

PHIL: Robert . . . I've got to eat shortly.

ROBERT: This man came in at lunch time . . . and he knew me.

PHIL: What?

ROBERT: He knows you too. He was a fascist . . . sent by the National Front . . . He wanted to suck me off . . .

PHIL: Maybe he was on a diet . . .

ROBERT: He must have been one of yours . . . who was he?

PHIL: Sounds like Eddie . . . the lover of my mother's paramour . . .

ROBERT: He frightens me.

PHIL: Don't worry . . . he's a psychopath.

ROBERT: I don't want to be pursued by your insane relations.

PHIL: We don't know for certain it was Eddie. My family doesn't have a *monopoly* on Edinburgh's psychopaths . . . you did well this morning.

ROBERT: Do you think so? I was absolutely quaking when I arrived. I was saying 'Robert . . . what have you let yourself in for . . .' I was sure she was watching me extra carefully . . . so I got the jeans on the same coat hanger just like you said . . . then I was stuck with this spare hanger inside my jacket . . . I felt guilty . . . my knees were racing . . . absolutely quivering. So I was just off to the loo when she walks right over to me and says 'Where are you off to?' and I says 'The loo,' and she says 'You've only just come,' and I says 'So?' Are you listening?

PHIL: Nearly.

ROBERT: And I says, 'I've been bursting all the way on the bus,' and she says, 'You just been, I was watching,' and I says, 'Oh no, I went to blow my nose on some bog roll,' and all the time I could feel it slipping down . . .

PHIL: What?

ROBERT: The hanger . . . and it was three minutes to ten. It was like being in an Alistair McLean movie . . .

PHIL: Ahhh.

ROBERT: . . . so I just pushed past her and went to the loo and whipped it out . . .

PHIL: What?

ROBERT: The screwdriver . . . and I took off the top of the cistern and shoved the hanger inside and screwed the top back on just like a bank robber.

PHIL: Did you flush it?

ROBERT: Of course . . . So I was back in the shop just as you came in . . . it was good wasn't it? What are we doing tonight? Let's go out and celebrate.

PHIL: I'm meeting up with Richard . . . this new guy at college. We're going to this German film . . . sub-titles . . .

ROBERT: Why didn't you ask me?

PHIL: I'm asking you now. Come with us.

ROBERT: I don't want this other guy hanging around. I want to go out to the Dragon Pearl . . . just the two of us.

PHIL: Do you fancy one of those denim waistcoats?

ROBERT: No!

PHIL: Come with us. Make a threesome.

ROBERT: No!

PHIL: I'm sorry, Robert. We'll go out tomorrow . . . go to the Loon Fung. Have you got any money?

ROBERT: I want to go out tonight . . . with you . . . alone.

PHIL: I can't.

ROBERT: I go off people so quickly.

PHIL: I'm just getting on with my life.

ROBERT: What about our life? I'm just company . . . someone to help pay the bills.

PHIL: We're companions aren't we?

ROBERT: I've started cottaging again.

PHIL: Friendships last longer than affairs . . . an affair . . . that's just playing games.

ROBRT: One of my punters took me to Nottingham a few months back.

PHIL: Not *the* Nottingham?

ROBERT: Yes! We went to Shades . . . and the Pavilion . . . had a great time together.

PHIL: You can have a good weekend anywhere . . . it's the weeks and weeks that are difficult. So what happened to your Nottingham friend?

ROBERT: Didn't really fancy him. He had money . . . but I've got my standards to look after . . . and you're still going with Richard tonight?

PHIL: Yes.

RICHARD *is out shopping. He has a bag of records that he's bought.*

RICHARD: Excellent . . . excellent! Pollini playing the Chopin Etudes . . . only £1.90 from Boots . . . I'm sure they got the prices mixed up . . . Solomon playing Mozart Piano concertos – a double album! . . . Wonderful performances . . . only £2.50 . . . what an excellent outing. Edinburgh . . . I take back all the rude things I've ever said about you! And Phil will be waiting for me this evening . . . at least I think he will . . . he will . . . of course he will. Now . . . I've just got time to get back to my lodgings for my tea . . . and then I'm away out again!

PHIL *is walking past the Haymarket towards Princes Street. He meets* PETER *the solicitor.*

PHIL: Hi Peter . . .

PETER: Ah . . . now then . . . where are you off to you naughty boy?

PHIL: Oh . . . I'm meeting this guy later on . . . I thought I'd call in at the Kenilworth for an hour or so.

PETER: Oh no you're not.

PHIL: Why don't you come? You can buy the drinks.

PETER: I've got a better idea. Let's go back to the office. We can raid the booze cupboard for nothing . . . and relax.

PHIL: Oh . . . no . . . I'm not on tonight.

PETER: Have you heard about my recital? I'm giving a recital next Thursday . . . to a selected audience at my flat . . . Lieder . . . Schubert, Mahler . . . and Wolfe . . . £2 a ticket in aid of SMG* funds.

PHIL: Have you sold any yet?

PETER: Of course. Not many . . . I have a following you know . . . they'll flock on the night.

PHIL: I've got to go.

PETER: Come back for a while. I've had a lousy day . . . conveyancing, debt collecting . . . and this bloody idiot complaining that leaves from his neighbour's tree are blocking his gutters. I'll make it worth your while.

PHIL: Do you promise not to invite me to your recital?

PETER: Right oh . . . consider yourself under contract . . .

PHIL: Just half an hour, mind . . . and no residual rights.

ROBERT *outside GHQ at the East end of Princes Street.*

ROBERT: Over there . . . the gents opposite the North British Hotel . . . that's GHQ . . . the busiest cottage in

*Scottish Minorities Group

Edinburgh. I'll be down there in just a minute. There's always a chance of scoring day or night . . . the chase quickens up around closing time. I'm surprised Chateau Charles isn't here . . . he's an institution . . . he's had more chickens than just about anyone in town. He'd follow me down . . . not because he thinks there's any chance with me . . . but just in case I've got something in tow.

ROBERT *has gone down into GHQ and is pissing.*

We don't speak down here. The game's played silently most of the time. We don't stay long either . . . the police keep an eye open. Well . . . I've run dry . . . adjust my dress like a gentleman. Nothing worth waiting for here. In and out's the first rule of cottaging. Never hang around and you'll not get caught. Mind . . . there is one guy who loves cottaging so much that he spends his entire annual holidays at it each year . . . travelling all over Scotland. He even takes a thermos and packed lunch with him . . . a sort of Egon Ronay.

I've had enough of trolling around . . . same bloody faces everywhere. I'm going to take a look in at the Traverse Theatre Bar sometimes get trade in there . . .

PHIL *meets* RICHARD *outside the film theatre.*

PHIL: Sorry I'm late Richard . . . I got held up . . .

RICHARD: Are you sure you want to go and see this?

PHIL: Yes . . . look . . . you buy the tickets . . . there's the money.

He gives RICHARD *a £5 note.*

RICHARD: I'll pay you in.

PHIL: No . . . no . . . I just got the cash specially. I want you to buy the tickets though . . . like taking me to the pictures. Do this for me.

RICHARD: Right . . .

PHIL: I want the change, mind . . .

They go into the cinema.

ROBERT *comes back to the apartment.*

ROBERT: This is the sort of evening that fills you with despair . . .

The Traverse Bar was flat. I got talking a few times . . . just casual punters . . . but I couldn't get interested. About once every two months I get post-pubescent menopause . . . that's the way I feel tonight.

Generally I don't bother with those theatrical wankers anyway . . . they're all into themselves. They try and talk all posh and intellectual as though they are where it's at . . . but underneath you get the feeling their Y-fronts could do with a good wash . . . and they're always broke . . . except for buying themselves drinks . . .

I never drink . . . only fruit juices and coke. I'm in training you see. When I score I like to know what's happening . . . and cope better than the other guy. I take a pride in myself. With the right man I can come all night . . . thanks to Coca-Cola.

At last PHIL *arrives back with* RICHARD.

PHIL: We've had a great time. This is Richard.

RICHARD: Hello.

PHIL: This is Robert. We share this place.

ROBERT: What was the animal film like?

PHIL: Don't take any notice. I'll make some coffee. You want any coffee, Robert?

ROBERT: Of course.

PHIL: Oh . . . Richard . . . do you like tartan shirts? Would they go well with these jeans?

ROBERT: Don't answer.

PHIL: Robert works in a men's shop . . . he gets things at cost price. Would you like a lumber jack's shirt, Richard?

RICHARD: I've never really thought about it.

ROBERT: Do you fancy that? I don't . . . I've gone right off it. I'm just his vassel.

PHIL: Why am I making you coffee then?

RICHARD: Nice place you've got here.

ROBERT: Your friend's got a sincerity problem, Philip . . .

PHIL: Two sugars, Richard?

RICHARD: Yes, please.

PHIL: Would you like to see my photographs? I was staying with this guy down in London. I answered this advertisement in Gay News. He had me to stay for Christmas . . . took me all over. Where's the viewer, Robert?

ROBERT: Don't bother.

RICHARD: Well I'd like to see them.

ROBERT: The batteries are flat.

PHIL: How do you know?

ROBERT: I took them out to use in the vibrator . . . they're finished . . .

PHIL: That's my vibrator you cunt . . . buy your own bloody equipment.

ROBERT: It was that deputy headmaster you introduced me to . . . Richard . . . he wanted to put me into a straight jacket next time round. Be grateful you didn't lose it. It scuttled up him like an Olympic mole . . . I thought it was going to be a hospital job at first. Are you staying here the night?

RICHARD: No.

ROBERT: Good! We share a room and I'm dying to get some sleep. Do you know what it's like to play twelfth man?

PHIL: You may wake up dead tomorrow.

ROBERT: How are you settling in at College, Richard?

PHIL: Oh, Richard . . . I'm full of work just now . . . there's so much to do. I haven't had a man for weeks. I'm right off men, in fact . . . till I've got my essays done.

ROBERT: Isn't it pathetic . . .

PHIL: Help me, Richard. I've got my assessment in two weeks. I'm in the opening five pages of *Waiting for Godot*. I'm playing Vladimir . . . help me . . . please . . .

ROBERT: He pleads like a little child when he wants anything.

RICHARD: You'll make a good tramp without my help.

ROBERT: Haaaaaaaa . . .

PHIL: I'll bring them to College.

RICHARD: What?

PHIL: The photographs. I'll get some new batteries . . . I'll show you at lunch time. I had a wild time down in London, Richard. I was in the Colherne one night . . . got picked up by this guy . . . all leather and chains with a chest like a door mat. I thought he'd be different. I went back to his place and he tried to murder me . . . he did . . . he picked up this carving knife and started waving it around . . . like . . . like Sir Alexander Gibson . . . then he pinned me to the bed and said he was going to punish me for walking the streets . . . then he wanted to piss on me and I got up and fled out of the room and flew into the Boltons and told the lads what had happened . . . and they laughed Richard . . . Have some more coffee? Would you like a biscuit?

RICHARD: I'm away home now.

PHIL: Stay a bit longer . . . I'm not ready for bed yet.

ROBERT: I am.

RICHARD: So am I. Thanks for the coffee. Goodnight, Robert. I'll see you again.

ROBERT: Really?

PHIL: Oh . . . well . . . goodnight Richard . . . I'll see you tomorrow.

RICHARD: Yes.

RICHARD *leaves.*

ROBERT: Good!

PHIL: I hate you. When do I go on against your friends like that?

ROBERT: I haven't got any friends.

PHIL: You know what I mean. I like Richard. He won't come back now.

ROBERT: Like a bet?

PHIL: Why are you so aggressive?

ROBERT: I hate being surplus to your requirements . . . discontinued stock.

PHIL: You're not . . . What have you been doing tonight? Why are you so bitter? I keep trying to please everyone. We're sharing, aren't we?

ROBERT: I want more . . . that's all.

PHIL: What more is there? You're going to walk out on me. Like all the others. You've got a good base here. You've got a job. A month ago you were lousy around the streets. What are you going to do? Go back to the Spider. He'll welcome you back.

ROBERT: I'm not going back to the Spider. No way. But I wouldn't mind taking another trip down south of the border.

PHIL: Don't leave me, Robert . . . not yet . . .

ROBERT: I'm not leaving right now.

PHIL: I'll make you another coffee. Don't move . . . I'll do it . . . I'll get you a nice present . . . would you like a lumber jacket shirt? I'd like one . . . let's do it tomorrow . . . ten o'clock.

ROBERT: No . . .

Evening. EDDIE *on the streets following* PHIL.

EDDIE: I was born in Tyneside . . . but I came to Leith with my mother when I was a bairn so I want to believe I'm Scottish through and through. Well I am! But I still go back to Newcastle once a year to visit my granny. She's ninety-three and lives off Westgate Hill behind these bike shops. There's a whole road of them there, you know. And swap shops. They have swop shops too . . . down there they do. Geordies can't afford to buy things from new. Not all the time like we do. They can't help it. I've got nothing against Geordies . . . I mean . . . it's not their fault is it? I've had a Scottish education and that gives you opportunities . . . you know . . . to think for yourself. To tell the truth I hate fucking Geordies. Except for my Granny. She can't help it either.

EDDIE *overhears the following scene with* SPIDER.
PHIL *is walking past the National Gallery.* SPIDER *accosts him.*

SPIDER: Phil . . . where are you off to?

PHIL: Hello Spider. How's things? I like your new wig.

SPIDER: You should have seen my curly perm. The lads kept passing me the dirty saucepans for weeks . . . and how's young Robert surviving with you?

PHIL: Fine.

SPIDER: He was special vintage . . . to me he was . . . lucky bastard . . .

PHIL: Special to me too.

SPIDER: . . . and he's got a job . . . an appropriate job, I gather. He still owes me for the shoes . . . £15. That's three nights he owes, Phil. There'll be interest to pay soon. Spider always gets his way in the end. You know that. Tell him I'm still waiting . . . and I have a lovely young thing staying at the minute . . . down from Aberdeen. You would enjoy him immensely. Brisk . . . elegant . . . with a heavenly bouquet. I have decanted him and am sipping slowly to the last drop. Why don't you come to supper one night? You can be the brandy. The boys would love to entertain you.

PHIL: I'm busy with finals at the moment.

SPIDER: . . . and you're going to run off and leave me . . .

PHIL: I'm meeting someone.

EDDIE *doesn't know which one to follow. He follows* SPIDER.

EDDIE: Poofs!

RICHARD *at the Dalry Road flat.* PHIL *is in the bathroom.*

RICHARD: A few days after the film, we spent another evening together. We had a meal at some Chinese place . . . the Loon Fung? Something like that? Lemon chicken . . . excellent . . . and we went for a drink afterwards.

He talked . . . the way he does. Then, at closing time, I was just going to drive him back to his place, when he goes and picks up a complete stranger . . . in the Kenilworth this was . . . and expected me to drive them both back to the Dalry Road.

I did.

I just couldn't bring myself to tell him to fuck off home himself. So when the three of us got back to his apartment . . . well . . . he just left me standing there . . . said he was too tired to ask me in for coffee. It was just simple rejection of me for the evening. He'd finished with me, you see. I didn't want anything from him. It hurt me.

The next day he's all over me again at college . . . wanting me to come round here for tea. First he's going to do his

Vladimir for me . . . then he says he'll leave it to the assessment . . . then . . . when I come here . . . he's got his full Vladimir outfit on . . . and I have to read Estragon . . . while he leaps around the room trying to remember his lines. He's only doing the first bit of the play . . . not the whole thing . . .

He's in the bathroom . . . changing . . .

PHIL *comes out of the bathroom. He has been cleaning himself up. He is still wearing his Vladimir trousers, but is undressed above the waist. He is drying himself with a towel.*

PHIL: What did you think?

RICHARD: Do you really want to know?

PHIL: Of course. I don't have to believe you.

RICHARD: No, you don't.

PHIL: So?

RICHARD: Sit down. There are three things that I can help you with. But you are going to have to start your production all over again.

PHIL: There's the other boy as well.

RICHARD: OK . . . well listen and see what you think. First of all, you've got a problem with this Faber text of the play. It's full of the most precise stage directions – telling you all the business . . . where to pause . . . what tone of voice to use. What that really amounts to is a record of a previous production. What you should do first is type out the script and leave out all the stage directions. Go through that script with your friend and try and discover its sense. If you are totally stuck, refer back to the Faber edition to see if it helps in any way . . .

PHIL: Could you type it out for us?

RICHARD: I could . . . but I'm not going to. You must do it. You'll learn something about the bones of the play.

PHIL: OK.

RICHARD: Secondly . . . you may decide that your tramp costume is what you want. But I'd like you to try thinking of circus people rather than tramps. Take a look at all those pictures that Picasso did of sad, tired, hungry clowns . . . blue period . . . you'll find what you want in the art section of your library . . . I've checked. Perhaps I mean circus people who have been forced out on the road . . . anyway . . . if you concentrate on the sadness and the humanity of the play, the comedy and the grotesquenenss . . . which is all you're giving it at the moment . . . will look after themselves.

And thirdly . . . do you want any more?

PHIL: Yes.

RICHARD: This is more personal to you. There's very little music in your voice. You don't phrase things imaginatively. You time the faster exchanges well . . . and sharply . . . but whenever you get a longer bit, you never give it time to breathe . . . to live . . . I don't get any feeling of a real person behind the words. Now . . . hold on . . . I'm going to buy you a record! It's of Puccini arias sung by Maria Callas. She plays a whole lot of different characters and characterises them wonderfully . . . it's the slight changes in tone of the voice . . . the way she phrases things . . . the way she is able to give meaning to the simplest . . . or what seem to be the simplest phrases of music. You can hear what interpretation really means. It's wonderful, Phil. To play Vladimir well, you've got to try to bring to the part the same intense illumination . . . to every bit of it . . .

PHIL: I'm going to get changed.

RICHARD: OK.

PHIL *doesn't want to say anything. He finds his clothes, which are scattered around the place and gets dressed.*

PHIL: Are you bored with me yet?

RICHARD: No.

PHIL: You're angry though?

RICHARD: I was.

PHIL: About last night?

RICHARD: Yes.

PHIL: Why?

RICHARD: You know why.

PHIL: I want to hear you tell me.

RICHARD: Just picking someone up. Leaving me on the doorstep.

PHIL: You could do that too. I'll get you anyone you want, Richard. Just tell me *what* you want . . .

He needed a bed for the night . . .

RICHARD: You gave him more than a bed.

PHIL: So?

RICHARD: It's rejection, Phil . . .

PHIL: I don't want to hurt you, Richard. Just don't be like all the others . . .

RICHARD: Why do you hate kissing?

PHIL: Me?

RICHARD: Yes.

PHIL: I . . . well . . . I don't hate it. There's only a few people I kiss on the mouth . . . my mother. I don't like it, that's all.

RICHARD: You'll suck someone off, but you won't kiss them. Is that it?

PHIL: Do you think I'm trash?

RICHARD: Sometimes. Not really.

PHIL: Richard, I don't fancy you sexually.

RICHARD: What's that got to do with it?

PHIL: I would sleep with you. If you wanted.

RICHARD: I don't.

PHIL: I won't hurt you again. Don't look at me like that! You don't turn me on, Richard.

RICHARD: So what?

PHIL: You're honest. I think you are. That's rare. It's worth something. It's not your body. There's nothing wrong with your body. I could get off on it. Look! You're not just another fucking punter! You despise me. You think I'm trash.

RICHARD: No.

PHIL: I am. I am. Last week this guy from London was staying at the North British. I promised to find him a boy. Me playing the pimp. I went round all the bars. No one young enough for Douglas was on. I kept phoning him at the hotel, telling him not to worry . . . not to go out . . . be patient. Then I tracked down Pip. He's just fourteen and I said please do this for me and he made me promise that I wouldn't leave him alone with Douglas so I promised and when Douglas saw Pip he was so excited! So pleased! I love pleasing people.

And he gave us both a drink and there we were drinking whisky and this man touching up Pip . . . unzipping him and me just looking on. And Pip . . . he's massive for a fourteen year old . . . and Douglas slides down Pip's jeans and he's amazed at what he sees, Richard. And he gets the bottle of whisky and starts pouring it over Pip's cock and Pip says it stings and we start to laugh and there's this guy lapping it up off Pip's cock and Pip and I are in hysterics. And I was feeling left out of things so I put my arms around Pip and started to pull myself off. And Douglas . . . he finished me off . . . and then Pip came in his mouth. And Douglas was so pleased! He really liked it, Richard. And he said he'd spend another night in Edinburgh. Edinburgh was a great city. And he wanted me to find him another boy for the next day. And he gave me £20 and Pip £10.

I really am trash, Richard.

RICHARD: Did you find him another boy?

PHIL: He left town, that night. On the sleeper. He'll be back. They all come back, Richard. So will you.

RICHARD: Are you sure?

PHIL: I'm interested in what you said about Vladimir. Starting again is hard, Richard. I have a date with Estragon tomorrow. We'll look at your pictures. I'll tell him what you said.

RICHARD: 'You're angry?'

PHIL: 'Forgive me.'

RICHARD: 'Come, Give me your hand.'

PHIL: 'Embrace me! Don't be stubborn!'

RICHARD (*rejecting him*): 'You stink of . . .'

PHIL: I hate garlic.

RICHARD: Sweat . . . whisky . . .

PHIL: I . . . quite like whisky . . .

RICHARD *leaves.*
PHIL *studies 'Waiting for Godot'.*
Maria Callas sings 'Principessa Lo-u-Ling . . . ' section from 'In Questa Reggia' (ALP 3799).

EDDIE *is walking the streets after closing time with a can of beer and a carry-out. He tries to the cross the road and is nearly run over.*

EDDIE: Poof!

He presses the button on the pelican crossing.

You know . . . if I hadn't been a thinker I'd like to have been an artist. At least I think I would. Hitler had the same problem. I'm going to write a book . . . one of these days I will. *The Vengeance of the Lone Wolf*. You see when I was a kid I always wanted to be a redskin. That was before I realised they were sub-human, of course. I know that now. That's what stops me writing it . . .

The pelican crossing starts bleeping and EDDIE *crosses the road.*

At the Dalry Road flat, PHIL *is having a bath.* ROBERT *is trying to tidy up.*

ROBERT: That deputy head . . . I only went with him for money. He gave me more than I would have asked for. He understands. He'll come back for more. No straight jackets though. You never know what'll happen with a new guy. It's just as well to have someone like Phil around. He knows the game backwards. He's been playing it a year or two longer than I have. I'm eighteen. I'm no chicken.

PHIL (*off*): Robert . . . Robert . . .

ROBERT: Doesn't it make you sick. He even needs me when he's having a bath.

PHIL (*off*): Robert . . .

ROBERT: What?

PHIL (*off*): Could you bring in the shampoo?

ROBERT: Where is it?

PHIL (*off*): On the table.

ROBERT *finds it and takes it into the bathroom. He returns.*

(*Off:*) Robert . . .

ROBERT: What?

PHIL (*off*): Come back . . .

ROBERT: I'm busy.

PHIL (*off*): Please . . .

ROBERT: Ohhhhh . . .

ROBERT *goes through to him.*

PHIL (*off*): Scrub my back.

ROBERT (*off*): Poor little boy . . . you haven't got your ducks. Would you like your ducks?

PHIL (*off*): Thanks . . . I said thanks . . . ahhhhhh . . .

ROBERT *re-enters.*

ROBERT: My first visit to Edinburgh . . . didn't know where to go. Didn't need to as it turned out. Chateau Charles spotted me half way down Princes Street . . . fox among the chickens. He had me the once . . . that first visit. It was what I came for mind. There's money to be made. Wouldn't you pull a guy off for £30? Well . . . £5? I've made £30 during the Festival. The price of everything goes up then. I mean . . . the Festival's bloody rent, isn't it? You've got to get your sense of values right. If an opera ticket's worth £15, a night with a highly skilled rent-boy's worth at least £50 . . .

PHIL *enters in his towel.*

PHIL: Robert . . . you've tidied up.

ROBERT: I've just re-arranged the mess.

PHIL: I'm happy.

ROBERT: Does that mean you're going to keep me awake all night?

PHIL: Don't be angry with me.

ROBERT: Leave me alone.

PHIL: Why do you go on rejecting me?

ROBERT: Me?

PHIL: I'll make you a coffee.

ROBERT: I don't want any.

PHIL: What would you like?

ROBERT: Nothing. Let's go to bed.

PHIL: O.K. We'll go to bed. Would you like me to read you a bedtime story?

ROBERT: No.

PHIL: I'll tell you one, then.

There are two single beds. ROBERT *undresses.*

ROBERT: I don't want one.

PHIL: Thanks for the denim waistcoat.

ROBERT: Stop crawling. I don't want to talk to you.

PHIL: 'No one ever suffers but you . . . I don't count.'

ROBERT: I've still got those spots.

PHIL: Let's see . . . ummm . . . heat rash.

ROBERT: They don't itch or anything.

PHIL: Do they come out to feed?

ROBERT: No.

PHIL: I'll give you a splash just in case.

His bedside locker is full of medications. PHIL *gets out the bottle of Benzyl Benzoate.*

I'll do it. Shake the bottle. There . . .

He rubs some into ROBERT*'s stomach.*

Now get into bed like a good boy. Oh no . . . my pills . . . a curse on NSU . . .

PHIL *gets out his bottle of pills and goes to the bathroom.*

ROBERT: There's rabies on the continent and it's moving northwards.

PHIL *returns with a glass of water and swallows his pills.*

PHIL: I'd rather foam at the mouth than pee glass. I get every bloody thing. Wait till you've had a dose front and back.

ROBERT: No thanks.

PHIL: Have you been helping yourself to my Esoderm?

ROBERT: Oh . . . it was that guy I met at the SMG meeting.

PHIL: I wish you'd get your own medications . . . and your own battries. North Sea oil's not going to bring down the price of crab lotion.

ROBERT: I thought Boots gave you a free bottle with every tube of KY you buy there.

PHIL: Who was he anyway?

ROBERT: Who?

PHIL: At SMG.

ROBERT: Holyrood Harry!

PHIL: Ohhhh . . . I don't believe it.

ROBERT: He's been chasing for months.

PHIL: What did he do for you?

ROBERT He's got this massive double-double bed, and I was doused with your Esoderm after a night with Fire Officer Jimmy. I told Harry I didn't want anything. He said he just wanted company for the night. He brought me coffee in bed. that was nice. I like being looked after.

PHIL: I look after you. I'm a one man canteen

ROBERT: So I left my Marks and Spencers nics on and told him to leave it that way. Then he started playing up and before I knew what was happening he was upside down and . . .

PHIL: Foul, foul . . . oh foul . . .

ROBERT: He loved it.

PHIL: Spare me.

ROBERT: . . . and he came all over my face.

PHIL: Ohhhhhhh . . .

ROBERT: . . . and he screamed as he came . . .

PHIL: No . . .

ROBERT: . . . like this . . . Aaaaahhhhhhhhhhhh . . . ahhh . . .

PHIL: And was Holyrood struck by vengeful thunderbolts?

ROBERT: . . . and he gave me £10.

PHIL: What? Harry did?

ROBERT: He wants me back again.

PHIL: It stinks. Stinks. The whole world is rotten and I'm rotting away with it. My bowels are full of itching powder. We're all on hooks . . . like bait on hooks . . . and we wriggle around while there's life in us and the hook tears . . . and the punters gather round . . . and we're eaten and eaten . . . and the rent we get goes on rent-food, rent-electricity, rent-bloody-everything. I'm dying, Robert. And I love it.

ROBERT: You're not dying . . . you're just a Scottish drama student.

PHIL: . . . and I've got to be Vladimir in a week's time. 'There's a man all over for you, blaming his boots on for the faults of his feet . . .'

ROBERT: I'm tired. Let's got to sleep now.

PHIL: I'll turn out the light.

ROBERT: Goodnight.

PHIL: Goodnight.

ROBERT: It's been a good day.

PHIL: Do we have any choice?

ROBERT: What?

PHIL: Is there any alternative to bloody rent?

The door bell rings.

Oh shit.

ROBERT: Oh bugger.

PHIL: Yours.

ROBERT: No . . . yours.

PHIL: That's half the Edinburgh Fire Brigade.

ROBERT: That's half the Lyceum Theatre Company.

PHIL *answers the door. It's* RICHARD. *He's been drinking. He conceals a bunch of wilted flowers.*

RICHARD: Sorry . . . sorry . . . I'm very sorry. These are for you.

He gives PHIL *the flowers.*

PHIL: Oh God. Come in.

RICHARD: I've been out. Oh . . . you're already . . . oh . . . is there some one here? Oops . . . do you mind if I sit down?

PHIL: You shouldn't have come, Richard. We've gone to bed.

RICHARD: Have you? Who? Oh.

PHIL: Just Robert and me. Robert's tired. So am I. Why don't you go home, Richard.

RICHARD: Home? Oh yes . . . I don't want to. I'm being honest with you. You don't mind me being honest? I'm sorry . . . I'm . . . I've been out.

ROBERT (*from the bedroom*): Who is it?

PHIL: See . . . you've woken up my friend.

RICHARD: I'm not a stranger. Why are you talking to me as though I'm a stranger?

PHIL *goes through to* ROBERT.

PHIL: It's bloody Richard. He's pissed. These are for me.

ROBERT: Oh . . . has he brought me any?

PHIL: I thought I'd let him bring you the deadly nightshade himself.

ROBERT: Send him home . . . please . . .

PHIL: I have a horrible feeling he wants to stay the night.

ROBERT: No . . . and that's my last word on the matter.

PHIL *goes back to* RICHARD.

PHIL: Robert says 'hie'. Where did you get these things?

RICHARD: They were discarded on the street. I brought them straight to you. I also have this . . . (*He produces half a bottle of whisky.*) . . . which I thought might help to pass an hour or so of this bloody night.

PHIL: Wait there.

PHIL *goes back to* ROBERT.

He has presented us with half a bottle of whisky.

ROBERT: That must be the meanest act. We're not worth a whole bottle. What further proof do you want? Send him away.

PHIL: Are you inciting me to cruelty?

RICHARD (*outside*): Can I come in?

ROBERT: No!

RICHARD: Sorry.

PHIL *goes back to* RICHARD.

RICHARD: All right . . . I'll go . . . you don't have to say it. I'll go . . .

PHIL: Robert's had enough, Richard. I don't want to cast you out into the streets. Have you got a car here?

RICHARD: Yes . . . yes . . . it's outside . . . that's . . . well . . . that's what I was thinking.

PHIL: I wasn't thinking anything. I just wanted to make sure you got home safely.

RICHARD: Look . . . would you . . . perhaps it's unfair to ask . . .

ROBERT *comes through from the bedroom.*

. . . but . . . come back tonight . . . to my place.

ROBERT: No, he won't. He's staying here with me.

PHIL: Robert, you're interfering.

RICHARD: No . . . no . . . Robert's right. I shouldn't have asked. I shouldn't have come here tonight . . . I'm . . . well . . . I was lonely . . . that's all.

ROBERT: . . . and pissed.

PHIL (*to* ROBERT): Why are you so fucking unpleasant?

ROBERT: How else am I supposed to protect myself from you?

RICHARD: I'll go now. Goodnight gentlemen.

PHIL: Wait . . . I'll get dressed.

RICHARD: No. You're staying here. I'm absolutely in the wrong in this. Robert . . . I didn't mean . . . I had no idea . . . I can't say it properly . . . but goodnight . . .

RICHARD *leaves.* PHIL *and* ROBERT *get back into their own beds.*

ROBERT: Come in with me.

PHIL: No.

ROBERT: I'm sorry about Richard . . . all your other punters are just punters. If he ever comes back I'll treat him better . . .

PHIL: What are you like?

ROBERT: Please Phil.

PHIL: Bloody hell!

PHIL *gets in with* ROBERT.

Shove over!

He turns out the light.

ROBERT: Oh God . . . I'm selling bloody jeans at nine o'clock tomorrow . . .

PHIL: Are you saying your prayers?

ROBERT: What are you doing?

PHIL: I'm dancing at eleven . . .

ROBERT: Serves you right you stupid poof.

PHIL: Don't walk out on me, Robert. I need you with me.

ROBERT: I won't. Not yet.

ACT TWO

ROBERT *is back at the flat on a Wednesday afternoon.* RICHARD *is having a bath next door.*

ROBERT: I only get one afternoon a week off and I like my Wednesdays to myself. Phil doesn't usually get in till 5.30 or 6. I've got the whole place to myself. That's good. I'm not used to having my own territory. Then Richard turns up. There's no hot water at his place in the afternoon so he's come round here for a bath . . .

RICHARD (*off*): Robert . . .

ROBERT: He's caught this off Phil . . . or is it something in me? Would I make my fortune as a baths attendant?

RICHARD (*off*): Please Robert . . .

ROBERT: Another pleader . . . what?

RICHARD (*off*): Can I use some shampoo?

ROBERT: Did he have to ask that? *Yes* . . .

RICHARD (*off*): Thank you.

ROBERT: Phil's been at his little games again. This time it's advertising in *Gay News*. 'Scottish intellectual youth with interest in urban blood sports seeks wealthy highland gentlemen.' That's gentle*men*, please note. He's had half a dozen replies. . . . most of them from south of the border . . . one from Arizona. Two replies came separately from two men living at the same address in Auchtertool. He's arranged a rendezvous with both of them at the same time and the same place, asking each to wear a red rose in his button-hole.

RICHARD *enters in a towel.*

You're smothered in my Denim talc.

RICHARD: . . . for the man who doesn't have to try too hard.

ROBERT: I wish you'd get dressed. Your flesh threatens me.

RICHARD: Oh. Sorry.

RICHARD *goes back to the bathroom.*

ROBERT: And that's Richard in a nut shell. Did it occur to him that I might like being threatened? I'm assuming that his unannounced arrival this afternoon was planned. He knew somehow that I'd be here and alone. But he's a born failure . . . and hard to get excited about. I mean . . . most men clean and hot from a bath . . . sprinkled liberally with Denim and swathed in an easily penetrated towel would arouse at the very least my curiousity. But Richard actually makes me angry. He won't speak out on his own behalf . . . from his heart. I mean . . . what goes on inside that man? What is he really after? I'm not coping with him at all. He's confusing me. Oh Richard, leave us in peace. Go back to Tyneside.

RICHARD *returns clothed.*

RICHARD: Is that better?

ROBERT: Not really. Let's say things we can understand. What do you want of me? Why are you here?

RICHARD: I came to have a bath.

ROBERT (*aside*): I can't talk to this man. (*To* RICHARD:) Why not read *Gay News*? There are record reviews . . . bits about the theatre . . . and other escapist twaddle.

RICHARD: How much do you make on the streets each week?

ROBERT: Don't talk to me like that.

RICHARD: You wanted me to talk about things we can understand.

ROBERT: You don't know anything about it.

RICHARD: I sell myself as a lecturer.

ROBERT: So?

RICHARD: I'd like you to come out with me tonight.

ROBERT: What?

RICHARD: We can have something to eat . . . go and see a film . . . anything you want.

ROBERT: I don't know what's on.

RICHARD: Does it matter?

ROBERT: It does if we're going out to the cinema. I don't know whether I want to go out. I don't know what I want to do. I haven't got any money.

RICHARD: I'll pay you in.

ROBERT: I don't know what Phil's doing.

RICHARD: . . . rehearsing his assessment . . .

ROBERT: I don't know.

RICHARD: I'll be in the K at 6.30 . . . if you want to join me.

ROBERT: I'll think about it. I'm not promising.

RICHARD: I'm not promising either. We'll leave it like this. *If* I'm in the K at 6.30 and you happen to come in and find me there . . . and *if* we want to spend the rest of the evening together . . . and *if* I've got enough money in my pocket . . . we *might* go and see a film.

ROBERT: . . . and have something to eat?

RICHARD: We'll leave it vague.

ROBERT: Yes.

RICHARD: I'm going now. Thanks for the bath.

ROBERT: Richard . . .

RICHARD: Yes?

ROBERT: Take care.

RICHARD: Yes.

RICHARD *leaves.*

PHIL *is outside his mother's apartment. He is carrying a bag full of dirty washing.*

PHIL: My mother lives here in Leith with this other woman . . . She's AC/DC actually. The pair of them are famous local personalities . . . they're known all over as 'Mop and Bucket'. It's true! Kids stop them in the streets down by the docks and ask, 'Which are you? Mop or Bucket?'

Home life was always a bit chaotic . . . it was great fun . . . this was when I was a kid myself . . . I wouldn't have missed a minute of it. My mother's Mop, by the way. When I tell stories about them nobody believes me . . . but they're all absolutely true. They fight all the time . . . moaning on at each other and busting the place up regularly. But they're inseparable. A few years back I was meeting this boy in Kenilworth . . . he was an art student at the university or something like that. Anyway, mother was still living with father at that time and I crashed right into mother and Norma, alias 'Bucket' . . . me and this other boy . . . I thought he was great because he has this white fleck in his hair and I thought how marvellous it was to have a white fleck in your hair and be so young and we always made love with the light on or in daylight so I could watch his hair bobbing up and down . . . we screwed all over the city . . . up Carlton Hill . . . in the rockery of the Botanical Gardens . . . on the top of a 37 bus . . . I was so innocent in those days. Anyway . . . back in the Kenilworth . . . mother stared at me and I stared back and saw who she was with and it suddenly dawned on me what was going on and I started to laugh and I went over and the four of us had a great time that evening . . . like getting to know your own mother all over again for the first time. She's great! She does my dirty washing once a fortnight and gives me tea.

ROBERT *is back at the flat with a punter,* THOMAS *from Harpenden, a teacher.*

THOMAS: It's a better paid post you see. I'm only on scale 2 in Harpenden. Did you go to school in Edinburgh?

ROBERT: No.

THOMAS: Where then? Where did you go? Oh . . . you don't have to tell me I suppose. Do you think I'm doing the right thing?

ROBERT: I don't know.

THOMAS: I like Edinburgh, you see. When I was training we used to come up here during the Festival. I helped on one of the fringe shows once. The students did this play . . . forget what it was now. Oh . . . *This Way to the Tomb* . . . someone called Duncan. I was the critic. I had to sit in the audience and shout out something at the right time. It was dreadful if the actors got in a muddle. I didn't know where I was supposed to come in. The audience was supposed to think this was an unsolicited interruption. Trouble was . . . I was the audience some nights . . . just about at least. It was terribly long. There were monks in it. This was before Ken Russell. God knows who chose it. Am I cheering you up?

ROBERT: No.

THOMAS: It doesn't matter.

ROBERT: Ohhh . . .

THOMAS: No really. You seem to be taking it very badly. I can't get it up sometimes . . . happens to everybody.

ROBERT: You're old. I'm only eighteen. I'm supposed to be in my prime.

THOMAS: Oh . . . this is your prime is it? I'm postponing mine as long as possible. Look. Don't be an idiot. It doesn't matter anyway.

ROBERT: Don't go on about it.

THOMAS: Then I got involved in this dance drama. That's what it was called in those days. I had to do this dance with this girl. Something about a night club . . . and taking her back to my place . . . a failed seduction. The audience howled as soon as I came on stage. The place was packed. I thought, God they're going to love this. We thought it was serious in rehearsals. They just fell about. The girl . . . she nearly collapsed with embarrassment . . . an ordeal by ridicule. We went through with it. By the end the audience was shouting and hooting. I mean . . . Fonteyn and Nureyev were a disaster compared with us. The students showered us with ferns and geraniums . . . the fresh soil still clinging. I was brought free drinks for weeks after. Poor girl had a nervous breakdown. Am I boring you?

ROBERT: Tremendously.

THOMAS: Do you want me to go?

ROBERT: Yes please.

THOMAS: But I don't want to leave you like this. There's no need to be unhappy. I mean . . . over what happened. We're not trying to prove anything, are we? I mean . . . I just came back with you for fun. And I've really enjoyed myself here. Well . . . if I get the job, can I make contact with you again? I may not get it of course. What the hell anyway. But I'd like to know someone.

ROBERT: I may not be here then.

THOMAS: You moving?

ROBERT: I haven't decided.

THOMAS *leaves a £5 note.*

THOMAS: Well . . . maybe I'll see you?

ROBERT: Maybe.

PHIL *enters.*

THOMAS: Oh . . . I'm just going.

THOMAS *leaves.*

PHIL: Who's that?

ROBERT: I can't remember.

PHIL: Are you glad to see me back?

ROBERT: Should we celebrate?

PHIL: . . . he didn't beat you?

ROBERT: Beat me?

PHIL: . . . but for me where would you be? You'd be nothing more than a little heap of bones at the present minute, no doubt about it.

ROBERT: Stop your blathering.

PHIL: Will you help me . . . please.

ROBERT: I'm not in the mood.

PHIL: Please . . . I'm practising my assessment. I need support, Robert. Do you know what this is? I only want you to read Estragon. Here . . . right at the beginning. It's not asking much.

ROBERT: I hate bloody plays.

PHIL: You've only got to read it. I've got to learn the bugger.

ROBERT: Pip came round.

PHIL: What? Why didn't you tell me?

ROBERT: I haven't had a bloody chance, have I!

PHIL: What did he want?

ROBERT: . . . said he wants to speak to you . . . I don't know.

PHIL: I don't want him round here. Christ . . . why can't people just stay out of my life? Everything piles on to of you. Damn this play. Get on with it.

ROBERT: You start . . . 'So there you are again . . .'

PHIL (*memory*): So there you are again . . .'

ROBERT (*reading*): 'Am I?'

PHIL: 'I'm glad to see you back. I thought you were gone for ever.'

ROBERT: 'Me too.'

PHIL: 'Together again at last! Get up till I embrace you.'

ROBERT: No.

PHIL: 'We'll have to celebrate this. But how? Get up till I embrace you.'

ROBERT: 'Not now. Not now.'

PHIL: 'May one enquire where His Highness spent the night?'

ROBERT: This is a pantomime . . . *Poof in boots . . .*

PHIL: *Dick and the beanstalk.*

ROBERT: *Hello Sinbad.*

PHIL: Get on with it.

ROBERT: In a ditch.'

PHIL: 'A ditch! Where?'

ROBERT: 'Over there.'

PHIL: 'And they didn't beat you?'

ROBERT: 'Beat me? Certainly they beat me . . .' Is this an S&M* production?

PHIL: 'The same lot as usual?'

ROBERT: 'The same? I don't know.'

PHIL: 'When I think of it . . . all these years . . . but for me where would you be? You'd be nothing more than a little heap of bones at the present minute, no doubt about it.' Did Pip leave a message? Did he look worried?

ROBERT: '. . . and what of it?'

PHIL: What did he say?

ROBERT: Nothing. I told you. Hurry up.

PHIL: 'It's too much for one man. On the other hand what's the good of losing heart now, that's what I say. We should have thought of it a million years ago, in the nineties.'

ROBERT: 'Ah stop blathering and help me off with this bloody thing.' It's daft this.

PHIL: 'Hand in hand from the top of Eiffel Tower, among the first. We were presentable in those days. Now it's too late. They wouldn't even let us up.' What are you doing?

ROBERT: I'm fed up.

PHIL: Why don't you help me? Just a little. I need help . . . Robert?

ROBERT: I'm away out with Richard tonight.

PHIL: Richard?

ROBERT: Yes. He came round for a bath.

*Sado-masochism

PHIL: What? What happens in this place when I'm away? I can't cope. I thought you hated him.

ROBERT: Oh . . . no . . . not really. I'm getting used to him now. I pretend not to like him . . . oh . . . it's not that either . . . but he's offered to take me out . . . that's kind . . . after what happened last week.

PHIL: Maybe he enjoys punishment. What are you going to do.

ROBERT: See a film. Go for a drink. I don't know. Talk?

PHIL: He'll whisk you out of the K into the coffee bar next door.

ROBERT: That's OK by me. What does it matter to you anyway? He's joined your growing pile of rejects.

PHIL: 'No one ever suffers but you. I don't count. I'd like to hear what you'd say if you had what I have.'

ROBERT: Oh God . . . not another dose.

PHIL: You're so close to me. I mean physically close. But you're nowhere. You hardly exist. It wouldn't matter if you came or went or vanished into thin air . . . because you don't realise or do anything to *help me, Robert*!

ROBERT: You're bloody mental . . .

PHIL: '. . . funny . . .'

ROBERT: Why don't you help me?

ROBERT *leaves.*

PHIL: '. . . nothing to be done . . .'

RICHARD *is in the cafe next to the Kenilworth.* ROBERT *is fetching two cups of coffee.* RICHARD *has been buying more records.*

RICHARD: This really is special! Furtwangler conducting Bruckner's 9th symphony in Berlin in 1944. I've heard this performance on the radio, but have never been able to get a copy of it. It's a live performance, and the orchestra and the audience must have felt that the end of the world was at hand. The result is so astounding that you should only experience a record like this two or three times in a lifetime. I found this copy in a dingy, anonymous shop, hidden in an arcade. It cost me one pound.

We hear the opening moments of the performance . . . (Polygram 2562 058). ROBERT *brings over two coffees.*

We didn't like the atmosphere next door in the K, so we've come in here.

ROBERT: I did London when I was sixteen. I was sick at first. Nowhere to go. So I headed for Piccadilly Circus . . . looking for punters. Well . . . somewhere to stay the night actually. So I stood outside this cinema with this lesbian film on. Whenever anyone got close I panicked. That was odd. I'd been on the game in Edinburgh, but London was different. I didn't know the territory, you see. Or the people. They're all bloody foreigners down there. Then I met this Chinese kid. He'd come from North Shields . . . all the way to bloody London. He'd got settled in. He took me to this boys' hostel . . . behind Leicester Square. The warden had made him a housemaster . . . or something. He was absolutely hairless . . . with golden skin . . . and butch as hell. I never looked back after that . . . had a great summer.

RICHARD: I haven't got that sort of . . . energy. Back in Newcastle I go to an occasional CHE* meeting. Sometimes I take a look in The Senate Bar. I never go to the Eldon . . . get's rough in there . . . sometimes at least. I'd rather keep myself to myself.

ROBERT: I'm bored with Edinburgh. I want to make a break, Richard. I don't feel at home with Phil.

RICHARD: You don't have to stay there.

ROBERT: When I was a kid I used to love pirate books. I've always wanted to be captured by pirates . . . you know . . . nice pirates . . .

RICHARD: Would I make a nice pirate?

ROBERT: You're not part of a crew, Richard . . . you're more like marooned . . .

RICHARD: Why don't you rescue me?

ROBERT: Can you lend me some money?

RICHARD: What for?

ROBERT: I owe someone some money, Richard. I'm in trouble. I've got to pay it back.

*Campaign for Homosexual Equality

RICHARD: How much do you need?

ROBERT: £25.

RICHARD: What?

ROBERT: I know it's a lot. What am I going to do, Richard?

RICHARD: Tell me about it.

ROBERT: Oh . . . it's this man . . . that's all . . . he lent me some money and he wants it back. I'm not safe around the streets till I've paid it. He's threatening me. I've got to pay him. I can do it tonight . . . I'll pay you back.

RICHARD: When?

ROBERT: At the weekend . . . when I get paid. You'll get it back, Richard.

RICHARD *gives him the money.*

RICHARD: That's just about cleaned me out for the evening.

ROBERT: Are you hungry? I'm starving. Let's go to the Dragon Pearl. I'll pay . . . you can be my guest for the evening . . .

RICHARD: Don't worry. I'll use my Access card.

ROBERT: You're a friend to me. I'm glad I found you. I need you, Richard.

RICHARD: Need me?

Carlton Hill. EDDIE *is following* ROBERT *and overhears the following encounter.*
SPIDER *tracks down* ROBERT *by night.*

SPIDER: Butterfly boy . . . a night flight to Carlton Hill . . .

ROBERT: Hello Spider.

SPIDER: What treats have you for me tonight?

ROBERT: None at all.

SPIDER: Come . . . let me look at you. Dear me. Bags under your eyes. You need old Spider to take care of you again. Your bright colours are starting to fade a little. Has the sweet butterfly become a night moth? Don't turn away like that. You used to come to Spider for comfort . . . and protection.

ROBERT: I've got to go.

SPIDER: And what have you done with those expensive shoes I paid for? Where's the money? You owe me money. £15. You know how to pay. We can settle the matter so amicably.

ROBERT: Leave me alone.

SPIDER: I'll burn your pretty wings. I want something now.

ROBERT: I haven't got any money. I'm broke. I'll pay you later.

SPIDER: I want it now. You don't need money to pay your debts. Don't let's waste time. The boys will be pleased to see you.

ROBERT *gives him £5.*

ROBERT: That's all I've got. I'll pay the rest later.

SPIDER: Empty your pockets. I'll get what's due one way or another, you little bastard.

ROBERT: Fuck off.

SPIDER: Ah . . . more money . . .

ROBERT: Give me that.

SPIDER *knocks him to the ground.*

SPIDER: That's another £10 I've taken. You've been doing good trade lately.

He throws the rest of the money back at ROBERT.

That's yours. Why not start a fresh account sometime?

SPIDER *leaves* ROBERT *groping around in the dark for the rest of his money.*
EDDIE *confronts* SPIDER.

EDDIE: *Cunt*! Robert . . . fuck off out of here . . .

ROBERT *gathers the rest of his money and runs off.*

Fucking queer cunt picking on wee laddies . . .

SPIDER: Let me go.

EDDIE (*taking the money*): I'll have this . . . and this . . . and this . . .

SPIDER: Be careful.

EDDIE: Spider . . . aye . . . I know who you are . . . been following you, haven't I. Taking money off wens. You leave Robert alone . . . never go near him again.

SPIDER: Ahhhhhh . . . Robert is it? Such a sweet boy . . .

EDDIE: Don't speak like that. Vermin . . .

EDDIE *is preparing to belt* SPIDER *but* SPIDER *has got out a flick knife. He swings at* EDDIE *and misses.*

Ahhhh . . . knives is it . . . come on pretty boy . . .

SPIDER *slashes again but* EDDIE *catches his arm. He is about to grab the knife when* SPIDER *stabs him in the hand, leaving the knife sticking there with blood pouring from the wound.*

Blood . . .

SPIDER *flees.*

Applause as PHIL *takes a bow as Vladimir at his college assessment.*

ROBERT *is alone at the flat. He has been sitting in the dark, as though hiding. The doorbell rings. It's* RICHARD.

RICHARD: Are you alone?

ROBERT: Yes. Come on in.

RICHARD: I come hot foot from Phil's assessment.

ROBERT: Where is he?

RICHARD: Catching the bus. He wanted to see his mother.

ROBERT: Was she there?

RICHARD: That's one way of putting it.

ROBERT: What was it like?

RICHARD: Odd. Competent. He has a good sense of timing. He reacted cleverly to the audience. He was performing to us, not concentrating on interpretation at all. It was certainly striking.

ROBERT: Has he passed?

RICHARD: I imagine so. Nothing to do with me. No one's interested in my opinion.

ROBERT: I am.

RICHARD: How kind.

ROBERT *is very affectionate.*

ROBERT: Would you like a coffee?

RICHARD: I feel really dark this evening. Don't move, Robert. I want your shadow near mine. There. I'm tired of college . . . and this city . . . and of bars . . . and wet streets. I really want to forget it all, Robert. I wish I was back in Newcastle tonight. I miss my own place.

ROBERT: So do I.

RICHARD: Aren't you happy here?

ROBERT: Not really.

RICHARD: How are you going to escape?

ROBERT: I don't know.

RICHARD: We're doing this Pirandello play at college . . . *Henry IV* . . . and it's difficult working out what's real . . . or perhaps . . . what's really happening . . . and what isn't. I feel like that right now. I don't know *how* you exist in my life . . . or what I'm doing here. What is holding us together, Robert? Or am I just making that up? Sometimes I think we're adopting each other like lost people. Perhaps we're brothers. You're my son. That's more realistic. Do you think you're my son?

ROBERT: I don't know.

RICHARD: If you're not, what on earth am I doing here? Why do we meet? We're not lovers. Sometimes we're not even friends. I need to understand things better, Robert. Otherwise . . . I can't go any further. I shall just become too aware of the hunger in your eyes . . . your unpaid bills. Why don't I give you money, like a beggar in the street, and just clear off out of your life?

PHIL *enters still dressed as Vladimir. This time his Vladimir costume shows the influence of* RICHARD *on his production. The costume and make-up are blue, beggarly and sad . . . as in a Picasso.*

PHIL: Oh Robert . . .

ROBERT: What a state.

PHIL: I'm a spent *force.* A shell. A husk. I have crossed and crossed the Rubicon. Behind me lies debris. A scorched land. And ahead . . . rejection and despair.

RICHARD: You did quite well.

PHIL: I know thee not old man. What does it matter? It's all games. Quite valueless.

Unless you've paid your subscription in full and pretend it has meaning.

Oh Richard . . . I've made a decision.

RICHARD: Oh . . .

PHIL: . . . about when I leave college . . . I'm going into business.

RICHARD: Oh . . .

PHIL: I'm going to make as much money as I can . . .

ROBERT: What sort of business?

PHIL: . . . so I can have a place of my own . . . my own tenement off George Street. I'm going to keep the phones ringing all over the city. I'll clean out all the cottages . . . the clubs . . . the saunas . . . I'll haunt every hotel lobby . . . every promising bar . . . until I've given my special list a complete overhaul. I'll start an account with a Building Society! I want a share in every monied punter north of Carter Bar. I'll feature on the Queen's New Year's Honours List for services to the Scottish Tourist Industry. I'll make the biggest impact on the balance of payments since North Sea Oil and Westminster won't see a penny of it! I'll start in Edinburgh, where the money is, and work outwards . . . through Glasgow . . . Aberdeen . . . I'll establish a network of rent-boys from the Clyde shipyards to the Cairngorms . . . from the oil rigs to the Outer Hebrides . . . I'll sponsor orgies in bankrupt stately homes and fly in Concordes full of foreign punters. It'll be my turn to screw the fucking rent!

ROBERT: Piss off and have a bath. Richard'll come in and scrub your back.

PHIL: Are you still my friend?

He goes into the bathroom.

RICHARD: Have you got the money you owe me?

ROBERT: Oh . . . not yet, Richard. Are you short?

ROBERT *is affectionate again.*

RICHARD: The spell is broken, Robert.

Outside the Golden Egg.

EDDIE (*off*): . . . and you can stuff your fucking eggs up your arse . . .

EDDIE *enters in his Golden Egg uniform.*

I've chucked in my job at the Golden Egg. You can't fry fucking eggs with half your hand cut away. I'll fucking kill the bastard. Fucking knives is it now? I just want to get away from all this shit. Edinburgh isn't bloody worth it any more. All cities are rotten if you ask me . . . queer bastards after your money. I think I'd make a great gamekeeper. When I was visiting my granny in Newcastle I went off with this kid ferreting. He had this ferret. Just kept it in his jacket pocket. And we caught this bus . . . going after rabbits. You just stick them down this hole and the rabbits come flying out and you bash their bloody brains out with sticks. And I was standing there with this bloody great club and this thing comes belting out of the hole and I bloody hammered it and hammered it . . . and killed it . . . it was the ferret. I love animals.

Crawfords tea room.

RICHARD: there are times in a man's life when all he needs is a string quartet. Oh God . . . I need one now. I want to run away to my own warm fireside . . . with a cup of freshly made coffee . . . and listen to the Italian Quartet playing Beethoven's Opus 135 . . . but instead I've got to face up to the reality of poor Robert, who knows my time here is running out, and who wants to meet me straight from work at Crawfords.

ROBERT: Can I come back with you? To Newcastle . . . when you go back?

RICHARD: No.

ROBERT: Why not?

RICHARD: I like living alone.

ROBERT: Can't you give me a lift down? I'll find my own place to live. There's too many problems with Phil. It's like having the blood sucked out of you. Take me with you. Let me stay for a while . . . with you Richard.

RICHARD: It's a rule I have about my life. Keep your own territory private. I've had people to stay. It doesn't solve anything. It just makes things more difficult. At the end of the day, people always end up by ripping me off one way or another.

ROBERT: I've brought you a present.

RICHARD: Oh . . .

ROBERT: Here. Take it.

RICHARD: Why?

ROBERT: Take it!

RICHARD *opens it. It's a lumber jack shirt.*

RICHARD: . . . yes . . .

ROBERT: Will you wear it?

RICHARD: Yes.

ROBERT: When you wear it, remember Robert from Edinburgh.

ROBERT *leaves.*

EDDIE *is in the streets with a canvas bag full of personal belongings.*

EDDIE: It's money really. I mean that's what it boils down to. I've washed my hand of Norma. She just uses me for money . . . that's all . . . and I don't like being used. She's a lost cause anyway. MacFerson's mother's got her fucking claws into her that deep. I'm leaving this city . . . but I'm not crawling out like some sort of rat. I'm leaving in style . . . first cass by British Rail . . . so people will remember me. I'm going down to London. But Norma's cleaned me out again. And British Rail isn't fucking cheap. There's this guy I met when I was in the navy. He's a bouncer at this place in Greek Street. I phoned him up last night. He may be able to get me a job . . . you know . . . as a heavy. Just seeing that people behave and respect the law . . . at the club I mean. Keep the riff-raff out. I'm travelling first class . . . when I've sorted out my business here.

Later.

PHIL: Write this down.

ROBERT: I've no money.

PHIL: What's that got to do with it? This is money you owe.

ROBERT: I can't pay it at the moment.

PHIL: Why not? What are you spending it all on? Coca-Cola?

ROBERT: I'm saving.

PHIL: Ahh . . . we share this place. Gas . . . £34.70. Write it down. Electricity . . . £18.20. Now add it up . . . go on. I want you to know what it costs to run this place.

ROBERT: £53.90

PHIL: What: £52.90. Don't make things worse. Divided by two. I said divided. Dear me . . .

ROBERT: I was away for five nights.

PHIL: I don't care about your seamy private life. Divided by two . . .

ROBERT: It's not fair.

PHIL: . . . a test of loyalty . . .

ROBERT: How can it be that much for gas?

PHIL: What? Oh . . . some of last quarter's bill was passed on.

ROBERT: Last quarter? I wasn't here for last quarter. Right . . . that's half off the gas bill . . . £17.35. The rest of that is your problem. Plus £18.20. £25.55!

PHIL: Rubbish. Are you trying to cheat me? Your friend?

ROBERT: Oh . . . £35.55. Right . . . half of that is . . . call it £18. I owe you £18. Is that fair?

PHIL: Where's the money?

ROBERT: Close your eyes like a good boy. There you are. Magic.

PHIL: I'll put it on the mantelpiece . . . and there's my contribution. Being an honest man, I concede you have a case concerning the extortionate gas bill. What's this? There's only £11 here. What about the other £7? You're trying to cheat me. *Me*!

ROBERT: I haven't got the rest just now. Can you wait till next week?

PHIL: What are you doing with all your money? You've had some off that social worker . . . some off the Fire Brigade . . . and the Bank of Scotland . . .

ROBERT: . . . very little off the Bank of Scotland.

PHIL: Get out on the streets. Take a trip to the Commonwealth Baths. Find a tourist. If you can't lay an American, retire! I want the money by tomorrow or you can fuck off out of here.

ROBERT: Do you mean you want me to leave?

PHIL: You've got a little behind . . .

ROBERT: I know . . .

PHIL: . . . with the rent.

The doorbell rings.

ROBERT: Yours . . . sweetheart . . .

PHIL *opens it.*
EDDIE *knocks him to the floor and bursts in.*

EDDIE: I'm going to fix you!

ROBERT: Christ!

EDDIE (*to* ROBERT): Where are you going, son? Remember me?

ROBERT: Don't touch me! I'll call the police.

EDDIE: It's him I want. That queer bastard.

PHIL: Who? Me? Eddie . . .

EDDIE: Trailing after us on a Saturday night . . .

PHIL: After you?

EDDIE: What's that money? I'll have that.

ROBERT: Leave that alone.

EDDIE: How much is there here? Where is it?

He starts turning the place over. He opens a cupboard door and a load of baked bean tins fall on top of him.

PHIL: Why not try the bedroom?

EDDIE: I think I will. It was my idea! You didn't have to tell me. You're coming too.

PHIL: OK . . . OK . . . I'm coming.

ROBERT *takes his chance and escapes from the flat and locks the door from the outside.*

EDDIE: Where's the money then?

PHIL: There isn't any.

EDDIE *pulls out the flick knife.*

Don't be mad? What would Norma say?

EDDIE: Where's it hidden?

PHIL: I told you. There isn't any. Robert's away for the police.

EDDIE: What?

PHIL: Get out while you can . . . and give me the money back.

EDDIE: Fuck off. You paid me this to screw you . . .

EDDIE *continues to turn the place over, discovering all sorts of equipment and porn mags.*

PHIL: Haaa . . . the police would die laughing. I wouldn't be fucked by you . . . fucking fascist bastard. I detest you and your pansy little friends camping around Rose Street. Get out of here . . . you shit-hole.

EDDIE: I only let Norma speak to me like that!

PHIL (*aside*): Where's the Special Branch when you need it?

EDDIE: Cunt . . .

EDDIE *finds the door of the apartment locked.*

Bastaaaaaarrrrrrds . . .

PHIL: Haaaa . . . you're trapped. You'll never get out now. Give me the money back . . . quickly.

EDDIE: Fuck offff . . . does that window open?

PHIL: Yes . . . yes . . . climb out of the window.

EDDIE: I thought of that!

PHIL *opens the window.* EDDIE *climbs out and sits on the ledge.*

Christ! We're two floors up!

PHIL: Jump, you coward . . . *jump*!

EDDIE: I'll fucking kill myself!

PHIL: Don't worry. They never cut the grass.

EDDIE: I can't.

PHIL: Use the drain pipe.

EDDIE: Where?

PHIL: There!

PHIL *takes the money and the knife out of* EDDIE*'s pocket and pushes him off the ledge.*

EDDIE: AAAAAAHHHHHHhhhhh . . .

PHIL *slams the window shut. The door is*

unlocked and ROBERT *enters cautiously.*

PHIL: Thanks, pal.

ROBERT: . . . what have you done with him?

PHIL *points at the window.*

Liar . . .

PHIL *waves the knife and the money at* ROBERT. ROBERT *opens the window and looks down.*

EDDIE (*off*): Bastaaaaaaaaaaaards . . .

ROBERT: Jesus!

PHIL: Dear me . . . still living?

ROBERT: Ooooohhh . . . Phil . . .

EDDIE (*off*): Fucking queer cunts. We'll hunt you down you bastards. You'll never be safe again, Philip MacFerson . . . never . . . *never* . . . we'll cut you up, MacFerson. You're a dead man. You'll be fucking trampled on, you queer bastards . . .

ROBERT *shuts the window.*

. . . trampled on . . .

PHIL: How diverting.

ROBERT: What are we going to do?

PHIL: What's new? The gutter's always been full of rats.

ROBERT: I'm going for the police.

PHIL: What? Keep off my territory. I may have a word with my Vice Squad friends.

ROBERT: . . . got to do something . . .

PHIL: Let's treat ourselves to new denim jackets . . .

ROBERT: *No*!

PHIL: Yes.

ROBERT: Impossible.

PHIL: Why?

ROBERT: . . . because I've hidden about twenty coat hangers in the cistern in the men's toilet. If I put any more in the bog'll never work and we'll really be in the shit.

PHIL: OK . . . forget it. What a mess everything's in. Let's get things straight again . . . back to normal.

ROBERT: What's normal?

PHIL: Like things were before.

ROBERT: That guy scared me!

PHIL: Eddie? He's always like that.

ROBERT: I've had enough. That's it. I've paid my dues. I'm leaving.

PHIL: When?

ROBERT: Now. I want somewhere I can relax . . .

PHIL: Relax . . . relax. I'll make you some coffee.

ROBERT: It's too late. It's finished.

PHIL: What are you going to do? Where are you going?

ROBERT: I don't know. Stop pestering me. You pester people! Did you know that?

PHIL: Are you still my friend?

ROBERT: Leave me alone.

PHIL: I want you here.

ROBERT: No.

PHIL: Yes.

ROBERT: No.

PHIL: Wait till the end of the week. We'll go to a party.

ROBERT *walks out.* PHIL *is left alone with the money and the knife and the chaos. The door bell rings.* PHIL *seizes the knife and stares at the door.*

PHIL *approaches the door. The bell rings again. He opens it. His father is standing there with a hold-all.*

MR MACFERSON: I found out where you lived.

PHIL: Come in. How?

MR MACFERSON: I phoned through to that college.

PHIL: Oh . . . yes . . .

MR MACFERSON: I suppose this is a surprise.

PHIL: Yes.

MR MACFERSON: Sorry, son . . .

PHIL: . . . not bothered.

MR MACFERSON: Sarah all right is she?

PHIL: She's fine. How's Jenny . . . Gavin

. . . Hamish . . . Nicky . . .

MR MACFERSON: Oh . . . fine . . . Simon's had the measles.

PHIL: Poor Simon.

MR MACFERSON: Sandra's doing her 'O' levels this summer.

PHIL: Oh . . .

MR MACFERSON: . . . runs in the family . . .

PHIL: What's that then?

MR MACFERSON: I was wondering if you would do us a favour, son.

PHIL: Oh . . .

MR MACFERSON: Look after this.

PHIL: What is it?

MR MACFERSON: Bits and pieces. It's got to stay out of the way for a while. I thought of you, Philip.

PHIL: Yes.

MR MACFERSON: . . . never visited you here. I thought I'd call round and see if you could help. I needed someone I could trust. Someone in the family.

PHIL: Am I in the family?

MR MACFERSON: I thought of you, Philip. That's all.

PHI: Are you up to date with payments to mother?

MR MACFERSON: Aye. Not quite. I will be when I've settled this lot. Has she been complaining?

PHIL: No. She never talks about you.

MR MACFERSON: No . . . well . . . can I rely on you then?

PHIL: How long?

MR MACFERSON: Maybe a month or two. No hurry at the moment. Let things cool off for a while. Will you do it, son?

PHIL: You've got to the end of the month to settle up with mother.

MR MACFERSON: Oh Philip . . . don't interfere. I don't need that. I only came to ask a wee favour. I thought it was about time you and I got together a bit more. There's always . . . things to work on. It might suit us both.

PHIL: It might. But as far as I'm concerned, this is business. Settle with mother.

MR MACFERSON: You'll not go telling her about this.

PHIL: No. I'll not interfere. Just sort things out in your own way. Pay what's due. That's the price I'm asking for storage space.

MR MACFERSON: Are you not pleased to see me?

PHIL: Yes. But this is business. Do you agree?

MR MACFERSON: Not a word to your mother?

PHIL: Agreed.

MR MACFERSON: Agreed. If you need to contact me there's a number for you.

PHIL: Right.

MR MACFERSON: I'll be away now.

PHIL: I'll make you coffee.

MR MACFERSON: No. I've other calls to make yet. (*He produces money.*) I was planning to give you this for doing it, but you've driven a harder bargain, you bastard. There's a future for you, son. I'll keep this for myself. You know there's a price to pay if anything happens to that stuff.

PHIL: Aye.

MR MACFERSON: Take care now.

PHIL: You too. Call again sometime . . . now you've found us again . . .

MR MACFERSON: Aye . . . maybe . . .

He goes. PHIL *picks up the knife again, closes it and puts it in his pocket.*

ROBERT *is hitching by the roadside outside Edinburgh.*

ROBERT: Come on . . . come on . . . Bastards! Thank God I've made a decision. With a bit of luck I'll be in Nottingham in a few hours. There's this kid down there. He's my age. We first met in the Turkish. I was laid out on this slab like a sweaty corpse. He was doing the massage. We never spoke. Then that nght I spotted him at Shades . . . said hello. He said he didn't recognise me with my clothes on. One of them will stop. So I phoned this kid up an hour ago. He's expecting me. It's great to know that there's someone there . . . waiting for you . . .

EDDIE, *bruised and bandaged, outside* NORMA*'s apartment in Leith.*

EDDIE: Norma . . . *Norma* . . . I know you're up there. I'll come and knock your fucking door down if you don't let me in. Norma . . . *Norma* . . . you whore . . . I fucking need you. I'm hurt. I'm bruised all over . . . *and it wasn't my fault.* For Christ's sake . . . I need you . . . and I'm not fucking pissed. For God's sake open the fucking door.

EDDIE *is soaked by a bucket of water.*

Oooooooohhhhhhhhhhhh Jesssssssussssssss. Right. That's it you cunt. You're really out of my fucking life for good. Right *out.* That's absolutely fucking *it* . . .

RICHARD *has arrived back at his place in Newcastle.*

RICHARD: My home smells damp. It's amazing how things go stale when a home isn't lived in. The kitchen has always been bad, mind. I put up a false hardboard wall to cover one side of it. It looks fine at the moment, but I know there's trouble just out of sight. Maybe I'll put in electric storage heaters to keep the place aired when I'm away. They don't need anyone to be there.

I found that my Access card was missing on the way home. I stopped off to buy petrol. There was no money missing. Just the card itself. I can't really believe that Robert was responsible. I don't think he had a chance to take it. I may have lost it. I don't know. I've got it insured against loss anyway.

Robert was on my mind all the way home. I nearly said on my conscience. He was beautiful. I thought so. I'd love to have taken care of him. Made a home for him. Put him on his feet. There was no future in it. I've seen it all before. They stay a week or two, then you come back one evening and find a load of your things missing and they're away. What's the point of asking to be ripped off?

Perhaps Robert was different. Perhaps I've missed something of real value in my life.

I'm going to have a hot bath and listen to some music.

If only I was sure that he had real affection for me. Me as a person . . .

Anyway . . . it's finished.

Music: Mozart Divertimento played by the Italian Quartet, the presto finale of Divertimento KV 136 (Phillips 65999 663).

THE RENTS APPENDIX

The RENTS Appendix

The earliest drafts of *Rents* were written in 1976. I collected stories from the real-life prototype of 'Phil MacFerson' and transformed these stories into short plays. 'Phil' and I would read these plays each evening, and he would challenge or approve of what I had written, and then provide further information. It was always my intention to fictionalise what he told me, right from the outset. My role was always that of playwright, not journalist or documentarist.

As a result of this process, and the many drafts that *Rents* has been through, there is a substantial residue of script. The *Rents* Appendix contains some of this material. I have selected a number of scenes that contain characters that are only mentioned in the final *Rents* script, including Phil's mother, Sarah, and her woman friend, Norma, who was formerly Eddie's lover. We also meet Jane Irwin, the provisional head of Charles Stuart College's Drama Department, where Phil is a student and where Richard Ridley is a temporary lecturer.

Michael Wilcox

The apartment of SARAH MACFERSON *and* NORMA *by the docks in Leith.*

SARAH: Rough cow . . . ah . . . hark at the ships . . . the sailor lads away to sea and the flags flying . . . I love the sailor lads . . .

NORMA: What's wrong with me?

SARAH: You're as daft as arse holes . . .

NORMA: I can dance the horn pipe too . . .

SARAH: Bagpipes more like.

NORMA: Fancy a drink around the docks after dinner?

SARAH: I'm away up town . . . I want some new shoes . . . I'm calling in on Phil . . .

NORMA: . . . and she thinks I'm daft! That son of yours should be put down.

SARAH: One more word against Phil and I'll bust your fucking arm.

NORMA: . . . I'm still the champ . . .

SARAH: You might be if you'd lay off the beans.

NORMA: . . . and I still love you . . .

SARAH: . . . then why do you let that Eddie hang around? Why? I'm sick of bloody Eddie.

NORMA: I was just waiting for that, you bitch. Do I go on at you when you go weak-kneed over bloody sailors. No. I let you be.

SARAH: Me and sailors is just romance. There's no danger in it.

NORMA: Eddie was with me before you were ever heard of . . . and he still cares for me . . .

SARAH: I care for you.

NORMA: A man's different.

SARAH: Who says he cares for you? I've seen him caring for our food, our electricity, our bloody everything. And where's the change of the £5 I gave you this morning?

NORMA: What £5?

SARAH: My £5.

NORMA: Oh . . . that . . .

SARAH: Aye.

NORMA: Spent it.

SARAH: What on?

NORMA: Can't remember . . . bus fares . . .

SARAH: What?

NORMA: . . . got to use money sometimes . . .

SARAH: Have you been meeting Eddie by any chance?

NORMA: We . . . bumped into each other . . .

SARAH: That's the last time I'm giving you one penny . . . thief!

NORMA: Who are you calling a thief?

SARAH: You . . . you smelly cow!

NORMA: Fuck off . . .

SARAH *hits her.*

Cunt!

NORMA *thumps her in the eye.*

SARAH: Ahhhhh . . . my eye . . . Aaaaaa . . . you've blinded me . . . aaaaaaa . . .

NORMA: Balls . . . let's have a look . . . oh aye . . . I have . . . Haaaaaa . . .

SARAH: It's all Eddie's fault . . . damn him . . .

NORMA: I had to give him the money.

SARAH: I don't understand . . . I don't.

NORMA: I won't do it again.

SARAH: Promise?

NORMA: Promise.

SARAH: Still love me?

NORMA: Aye.

SARAH: I'll make you a coffee.

NORMA: I'll do it . . . you lie there . . .

* * *

PHIL *is visited by his mother.*

PHIL: Oh . . . mother . . . come in . . .

She enters.

SARAH: Who was that on the stairs? What a bloody mess. I've brought you some stuff . . . coffee . . . six cans of beans. That Norma's got no imagination, son . . . the problems I have with her . . .

PHIL: Where did you get your black eye?

SARAH: The town's jam packed. I saw your father last week.

PHIL: Ohhh . . . I'll make you some coffee.

SARAH: He was with his latest bit. I quite fancied her myself. The bairns are fine . . . Jackie's had the measles . . . best time to get them when you're young.

PHIL: Did father do that?

SARAH: What! I'd bloody murder him if he raised a finger . . .

PHIL: How's your Norma?

SARAH: Flat out on her back. You should have seen her lying there when I left the house . . . moaning peacefully on the divan. She was snoring musically . . . like the space ship in *Close Encounters*. Oh Phil, son, I'm worried.

PHIL: There's your coffee . . . tell me.

SARAH: She's still seeing Eddie . . . giving him money and that. I keep thinking it's over between him and her . . . but then it flares up again.

PHIL: Maybe she needs a man occasionally.

SARAH: They don't screw or anything . . . they gave that up long ago. If that's what she was getting I'd understand . . . but it's something else . . . something I want to give her. I try . . . but she's not the easiest person to live with. What can I do about Eddie?

PHIL: Be patient. Let it play itself out.

SARAH: Why not force a showdown . . . him or me?

PHIL: You might lose.

SARAH: Have you been around the town much?

PHIL: . . . too busy with work, mother.

SARAH (*aside*): He's a bloody liar, my son, you know. There's times I've wondered whether he knows what's true and what isn't . . . but I love him . . . Phil's great . . . and if any of you buggers say a word against him I'll massacre the lot of you! But he is a bloody liar.

PHIL: I'm having trouble with this boy . . . I'm worried sick.

SARAH: What's he look like?

PHIL: Oh . . . Barbara Windsor without the tits. He follows me around the streets . . . he's going to get me into serious trouble, mother. If I go into a bar he appears from nowhere. I buy him a drink sometimes. His name's Pip . . .

SARAH: Pip!

PHIL: . . . lemonade . . . he doesn't touch anything else . . . oh . . . he loves nuts and crisps . . . and ice cream. We went swimming in the Commonwealth Baths. He followed me into one of the showers . . . there are a few cubicles with showers in there . . . and he starts wanking himself off. It's a problem, mother. I don't fancy him at all . . . he's a nuisance to my life . . . he's a pest. I'm thinking of taking advice from the student welfare service.

SARAH: Don't trust those buggers.

PHIL: He thinks he's got the pox . . . I can't see anything wrong but I'm taking him to the clinic for a check up.

SARAH: That's wise. Don't take chances.

PHIL: . . . and I'm behind with my washing. Can I bring it over at the weekend?

SARAH: Aye. We'll cook you lunch on Sunday.

PHIL: Are you staying for your tea?

SARAH: No . . . no. I must get away for the bus. What are you doing tonight?

PHIL: Oh . . . I'm going to see this film with Richard.

SARAH: Who's he?

PHIL: He's come to take a few classes.

SARAH: Oh . . . well . . . look after yourself, son.

PHIL *kisses her on the lips.*

PHIL: See you Sunday . . .

SARAH: Aye . . . take care.

PHIL: 'bye . . .

SARAH: Be happy . . .

PHIL: I'll try . . .

SARAH: 'bye . . .

PHIL: 'bye . . . give my love to Norma.

SARAH: I will . . . ca' canny now . . .

PHIL: Take care.

SARAH: I will.

She leaves.

* * *

PHIL *is back at his flat with* TONY, *another punter, a fitter in the Clyde shipyards.*

TONY: Who is this Robert you're sharing with anyway?

PHIL: Picked him up outside the cottage by the National Gallery. He was hanging around so I went up to him and asked if he wanted a drink . . . he told me to piss off. I had to chase after him and ask him three times before he surrendered. This was four weeks ago . . . just after your last tour of duty. I brought him back and made him one of my famous spaghettis . . . he's been here ever since.

TONY: I've brought you a present.

PHIL: Ohhh . . . for me?

TONY: There you are.

It's a Glen Campbell LP.

PHIL: Thanks Tony.

TONY: What's the time?

PHIL: . . . half five . . . are you travelling back to Glasgow tonight?

TONY: Aye . . . I'm taking the wife to the cinema . . . *The Thirty Nine Steps.*

PHIL: Better not be late . . . when are you coming through again?

TONY: Don't know . . . when I feel like it. Is that all right?

PHIL: I've got a full diary at the moment. I've got all these essays to do. They should have been handed in last term.

TONY: What is it?

PHIL: Oh . . . a project on children's stories . . . and this is the only extant manuscript of MacFerson on Ibsen. They all go in my assessment file . . .

TONY: You must be bloody mad. Get yourself a job.

PHIL: Where do you live in Glasgow anyway?

TONY: No questions. No business of yours . . . better this way . . . being strangers except when we're together. I want to leave my life over there . . . not bring it with me. I look forward to coming through . . . makes a change from drinking with the lads and all the Rangers talk driving you stupid . . . and the wife wanting this and that. Just think of me as another tourist. Got to go . . . 'bye . . .

He leaves.

PHIL: God . . . the things I've done for the Scottish Tourist Industry . . .

* * *

SARAH *enters her flat in Leith.* EDDIE *has been tracking her silently up the stairs and sneaks into the flat.* NORMA *is sleeping in the next room.*

SARAH: Eddie . . . get out of here.

EDDIE: You never even saw me . . . ha . . . I tracked you . . . followed you up the stairs.

SARAH: Get out!

EDDIE: Why shouldn't I come round? Nothing new about it . . . she misses me.

SARAH: Oh aye . . . ever since this morning. We weren't expecting you . . . that's the difference. She's sleeping and you'll not go disturbing her . . . not with me standing by. Why can't you leave us alone?

EDDIE: Us? What about me? Makes me sick . . . bloody women together. You make my stomach turn over . . . draining the life out of her. We were together once. You've turned her against me, Sarah MacFerson.

SARAH: Rescued her, more like. What do you want? Money?

EDDIE: Aye . . . if you've got some.

SARAH: No way.

EDDIE: I'll get myself away . . . I'm busy in the town tonight.

SARAH: I bet you are. You've had some off me today already, thanks to that soft cow. Aye . . . I've heard about you and her this morning painting the walls red in Crawfords . . .

EDDIE: Give us a feel till Friday . . .

SARAH *takes hold of his balls and squeezes tightly.*

SARAH: There's not one penny more you'll get out of me . . .

EDDIE (*in agony*): All right . . . all right . . .

SARAH: . . . and don't you try threatening me, you squirt. Now get out of here and don't come back uninvited.

She leads him out to the door by the balls and throws him out.

EDDIE (*off*): I'm not through yet, you fucking bent bitch!

NORMA (*off*): Aaaahhhhhhhh . . .

SARAH: If it's not one it's the other. What's up with you?

NORMA (*entering*): What's the time?

SARAH: Early. I'll bring you coffee.

NORMA: Eddie's coming round later . . . said he might anyway . . . I'm hungry.

SARAH: Tin opener's in the drawer.

NORMA: I'm too tired.

SARAH: Go back to sleep then.

NORMA: Get lost!

SARAH: Phil sends his best wishes.

NORMA: Fastest dick in the West.

SARAH: How do you know?

NORMA: What are we doing tonight?

SARAH: I'm having a bath . . . grabbing something to eat . . .

NORMA: I want a bath.

SARAH: Plenty of water isn't there? Then I'm back in the town.

NORMA: Again?

SARAH: Need the money don't we . . . with you supplying your menfolk. The money's supposed to travel in the other direction, in case you hadn't realised . . .

NORMA: Can I have the first bath please . . .

SARAH: Let's have one together . . . I'll be Moby Dick . . .

NORMA: More like Jaws meets Godzilla . . . with you in there's no room for the water.

SARAH: Ha . . . who's the little mermaid?

NORMA *races off to the bathroom.*

NORMA: First come . . . first served.

SARAH *races after her.*

• • •

SARAH is looking for punters in Rose Street.

SARAH: Rose Street's getting more like Sodom and Gommorah every night. It's something to do with blocking off the traffic if you ask me. The Go-Go dancers will be on later . . . that's usually good for a bit of trade. They're bloody useless dancers most of them. I may be a bit overweight but my God I could show those jumped up little tarts a thing or two!

* * *

NORMA *is massaging* EDDIE*'s back at home in Leith.* EDDIE *is lying flat on his stomach, being pummelled by* NORMA. *He is only wearing a black, studded jock strap.*

NORMA: Don't say I don't do things for you because I do . . .

EDDIE: Ummmm . . . Ohhhhhhh . . . ohh . . .

NORMA: I'm a bloody mother and wet-nurse and it's all favours because I could really do without you now but you won't leave me alone so here I am bloody doing for you . . .

EDDIE: I don't need mothering . . . I want . . . ahhhhhh . . . other things . . .

NORMA: Like what? That's all finished with as far as I'm concerned. We cook for you . . . wash your bloody clothes . . . you screw money out of us and we fight over it. We shed blood for you, you bastard.

EDDIE: Blood?

* * *

Charles Stuart College. PHIL *has been called out of a fencing class by* JANE IRWIN, *the Head of the Drama Department. He is fully equipped and has pinned* RICHARD *to the wall of the corridor with his foil.*

PHIL: I want you to give me advice, Richard. I'm concerned about Pip you see.

RICHARD: Will you behave yourself.

PHIL: He's a nobody in my life. He hardly existed among all those punters. His ghost has cornered me, Richard.

RICHARD: If you don't let me go I'll smack your bottom . . . ahhhh . . .

PHIL: He's becoming a threat . . .

RICHARD: Someone's coming . . .

PHIL: . . . he just sneaked in unnoticed . . . out of the shadows. I didn't realise he was dangerous.

RICHARD *manages to get the point of the foil away from him.*

RICHARD: Look . . . come round here. Can't you be serious for a moment?

PHIL: There was at least the possibility that he had got the clap, so I took him to the clinic and introduced him. I'm on christian name terms with the staff . . .

RICHARD: I bet.

PHIL: . . . Pip was delighted. He regarded me as his conquest you see. The swabs and probing of the VD clinic were an official recognition of his new status. And I was driven by jealousy along the corridor to the student counsellor. I know it was mad but I've never been recorded in the annuls of student welfare before. Richard . . . Vladimir is stalking me to beat me with my assessment. Now Jane wants to see me. What do I do?

RICHARD: You go and see Jane. Then you get on with your bloody work.

RICHARD *goes away.*

PHIL: Are you walking out on me?

PHIL *knocks and enters* JANE*'s office.*

JANE: Come in . . . sit down Philip.

PHIL: You've dragged me out of fencing class. I like fighting masked men. You can't be let loose in Scotland's schools unless you know how to handle a rapier.

JANE: Some days ago a report was passed on to me in strictest confidence by the student counsel service. I realise that you discussed a matter of some delicacy . . . but the arrival of such information on my desk demanded that I should pass on the dossier . . . in the strictest confidence . . . to higher authorities . . .

PHIL: What?

JANE: I have invited a representative from the Education Office to visit me.

PHIL: What is this dossier?

JANE: A relationship with a boy at one of the city's schools . . .

PHIL: What does that mean exactly? A relationship?

JANE: Oh come on . . . writing sick notes for a fourteen-year-old so he can visit the clinic during school hours . . .

PHIL: My discussion with the student counsellor was supposed to be off the record.

JANE: The matter was naturally referred to me as your course director.

PHIL: Acting course director.

JANE: Don't play with words.

PHIL: She had no right to pass on information without asking me first.

JANE: It is only right that the boy's headmaster should be informed.

PHIL: You'll make a total fool of yourself.

JANE: Don't interrupt. I've reached a decision.

PHIL: I was only testing the Student Counselling Service as part of my research for one of your over-due Course Work essays. I'm doing a study of school and college administration. There is no truth in the story.

JANE: I've checked with the clinic.

PHIL: Untrue. Their files are secret even from the police. You're bluffing you bitch.

JANE: What are you doing next year?

PHIL: You know that.

JANE: You may apply to Murray House but I'll see that your application is not accepted.

PHIL: Where is this man from the Education Office anyway?

JANE: Not here. Not yet.

PHIL: I want to tell him about you, Jane Irwin. You playing the rent game with your students. I wrote one sick note. What do you want? Fourteen-year-olds going round with the pox? You try it. I'll bugger your career if you force me into it.

JANE: Get a job south of the border . . . away from here.

PHIL: Exile? Never. They're all fucking queens. I've shown you the way out of this. This man you've sent for . . . find something else to talk about. I've still got your notes to Willy Hardy . . . the film fund . . . ? Terry Purdie? . . . Adrian's photographs? . . . now I'm going back to nail my masked friends.

* * *

The apartment of SARAH *and* NORMA *in Leith.*

SARAH: Keep bloody Eddie in order. Do you hear?

NORMA: Pussy's in heat is it, pet?

SARAH: There's no way Eddie's going to chase around after my Phil and his friends being a fucking nuisance.

NORMA: Stop nagging.

SARAH: I'm not. I'm just telling you. I'm not picking fights. I just want a quiet life . . . peace . . . a roof over my head . . . someone close at hand when I need them . . . someone to look after. I don't seek fights, but I'll look after my own.

NORMA: Eddie's his own master.

SARAH: . . . and where's the rent money?

NORMA: I paid it.

SARAH: That was last month's . . . overdue by weeks. I need £20 for this month.

NORMA: There's no money coming from me till next week.

SARAH: Next week's too late. The landlord won't wait.

NORMA: He'll bloody have to.

EDDIE *enters. He has a bag full of dirty clothes.*

EDDIE: Heil Norma!

SARAH: Shit!

EDDIE: I've brought my washing round.

SARAH: Do it yourself.

NORMA: I helped you with Phil's last week. Roll your bloody sleeves up.

EDDIE: If I had my way we'd round up all the bloody poofters in town and get them to do all the dirty washing. That's a good idea.

NORMA: Sling it over there.

EDDIE: I'd have the buggers painting the Forth Bridge . . . and building motorways . . . and scrubbing the Scott Monument. . .

SARAH: I still need that money . . .

EDDIE: . . . and I'd make them lick the bird-shite off John Knox's head. I'm full of ideas . . . original ones . . .

SARAH: Let's see in your purse.

EDDIE: If I hadn't been a thinker, I'd like to have been an artist. At least I think I would. Hitler had the same problem. Are you short of money?

SARAH: She's tight and mean and greedy.

NORMA: Why?

EDDIE: I can get you some. There's plenty of scum just waiting to hand it over. I'm setting up my own social service. Robbery. I don't carry cash around with me. Not with law and order and discipline being what it is. But I can get it if you want. I've no problem with money now. There's rates for it . . . if you want to borrow some. You see . . . I know how to look after my own. I'll not say more . . . letting the cat out of the bag and the horse bolt . . . he . . . that's nearly poetry . . . there's a future . . . providing we prowl the streets together. I've always liked bands. When I was a bairn I used to follow the Boys Brigade. The way they blew their bugles brought tears to my eyes. There's a lot to marching. It's called Unity . . . or something like that. Then we'll smash the money lenders . . . that's called philosophy. If you need some cash quickly, you've only got to ask. I'll want it back, mind.

* * *

NORMA *and* EDDIE *in the apartment in Leith.*

EDDIE: . . . so that's £55.32 you owe me . . . I'll overlook the pence . . . plus £7 interest . . .

NORMA: Screw the interest. Where are you living now? Why don't you leave me your address?

EDDIE: Quit nosing into my life. Anyway . . . there's no home for me here with that all-in wrestler of yours.

NORMA: Watch your tongue.

EDDIE: Get rid of her. Kick her out. This week . . . well . . . at the end of the month. Action now. That's my motto. Norma . . . we've got to smash socialism.

NORMA: What?

EDDIE: Penetration into the enemy . . . then . . . in the darkness . . . knives!

He produces a flick-knife.

NORMA: What the fuck are you doing with that?

EDDIE: It's part of my hidden strength. Never let the enemy know where the strike is coming from. Then storm him . . . without mercy. They ought to supply these free on the National Health to everyone who hates socialism.

NORMA: Give me that!

She grabs it from him.

EDDIE: Give it back. It's mine.

NORMA: Stop whining.

EDDIE: I want my knife back.

NORMA: Bastard . . . without a heart . . . always a curse to me . . .

EDDIE: Fuck off.

She hits him in the face. EDDIE *nearly explodes before subsiding.*

NORMA: And you would have me throw out my Sarah.

EDDIE: She's turned you against me.

NORMA: I'm not against you. I'm for you. You need to be taught a lesson so you won't let me down. There's no need for all your wild talk and being led astray. It's you that's left me. Really you have. I need Sarah and I don't want to lose her. She's the best I can do now. It's years, not months, we've been together. You can't keep losing everything. Not all the time.

EDDIE: It's me you're losing and you don't care. You fucking hurt me! I want my knife back. I can easily get another.

She gives him back the knife.

* * *

SARAH *and* NORMA *at Leith.*

SARAH: Either you stop seeing Eddie or I quit.

NORMA: You're interfering. I don't like that, Sarah MacFerson. Leave my life alone.

SARAH: Your life. It's our life or it's nothing.

NORMA: Bugger off out of here. I'm sick of all your complaining.

SARAH: . . . and you bloody drink too much. That's my earnings you've been drinking away.

NORMA: I told you what to do. What's keeping you?

SARAH: God knows. You don't know what you're saying. How will you cope without me?

NORMA: You? Just try me. I'll bloody cope. Eddie and me lived here before you split us. Now it's your turn. You get out and find a home for yourself elsewhere.

SARAH: You fucking cow.

NORMA: Don't you fucking cow me, you fucking cow.

SARAH: Screw you!

SARAH *storms out.*

* * *

Hours later. The Leith flat. NORMA *is miserable.* SARAH *enters.*

NORMA: Look who's landed.

SARAH: I've just come to fetch some things. Don't get excited.

NORMA: Like what?

SARAH: Close your eyes.

She fetches her money from its hiding place.

NORMA: Can I open them yet?

SARAH: Aye.

NORMA: Who's a clever bitch then?

SARAH: Me.

NORMA: Where are you going?

SARAH: Away.

NORMA: Where to?

SARAH: I don't know. Wester Hailes?

NORMA: Stay on. Might as well.

SARAH: Might as well.

NORMA: I'm sorry.

SARAH: I'll make some tea.

NORMA: . . . love it . . .

SARAH: What are you doing tonight?

NORMA: Nothing.

SARAH: We'll have a night on the town.

NORMA: What with?

SARAH *waves the money.*

I love you.

* * *

ROBERT *talking about himself. (This is the earliest* Rents *fragment from which the whole play grew. M.W.)*

ROBERT: That guy that wanted to put me in a straight jacket . . . he's the deputy headmaster of one of your Edinburgh Secondary Schools. Rate payers have their money grabbed so he can keep an eye on the senior boys. Only went with him for money . . . didn't take too much off him . . . just a few quid . . . in fact he gave me more than I would have asked for. He understands, you see, and will probably want to come back for more some time. You can never be sure what'll happen with a new guy so its just as well to have someone around like Phil . . . anybody really . . . but Phil knows the game you see like no one else I know. He's been playing it for a year or two longer than I have . . . I'm still only eighteen . . . I'm well hatched out. But Phil . . . there's not a bar, a cottage or meat rack anywhere in the city that he doesn't know. Not that he spends all his time searching for custom . . . doesn't need to. He finds what he wants and does a good line in phone numbers. He's made it his market, not the other guy's.

I started hanging around when I was fifteen and once I began to break through I had a crazy time for six months . . . I was astonished at the sort of custom I had with all these men, coming all over me in the most unlikely situations. Christ . . . if a guy took me to the cinema, I'd go out to the bog with him during the advertisements and let him screw me. Never got caught or anything . . . some of the guys that came in must have realised what was going on . . . but they just went blind to the whole business. Anyway . . . I just couldn't stop myself. It wasn't the sex or the pleasure of it exactly . . . it was seeing a grown man that I most likely despised getting that excited about me . . . my body . . . and feeling the tension and the sweat of him when he came . . . and his dejection as he cleaned himself up with bog roll after . . . the fear in his eye. Hatred in me gave me my satisfaction . . . and the power. I knew they were using me and didn't give a shit about me and I wanted to be sure they paid for it one way or another. One man punched me in the mouth when I laughed at him . . . I had more respect for him after that and went with him a few times . . . which was unusual.

For good times I went with younger men or lads of my own age . . . the beauty and pain exploding inside me. Christ . . . that's something I've lost now . . . I keep searching.

This is a game for bastards. I know. I've had a few and I'm fast becoming one myself. Like Chateau Charles . . . that's his name . . . He hangs around cottages and specialises in young boys . . . you can often see him at the East end of Princes Street near GHQ . . . any night in the summer just waiting there . . . usually in his shirt sleeves. He knows just how to pick them out and how to talk to them and before they know it they're away in his car with their trousers down and Charles sucking them wild. Fox among the chickens. The lads ask for it. I know I did when he had me. But what are the boys to do? Even the slowest of them know they've got pricks by the time they're sixteen and they see their mates going off with the girls but they *know* they're not interested so what are they to do, for God's sake? They don't want to spend the rest of their lives pulling themselves silly.

So a lot of them go to the toilets to see what they can find and before they've had time to wipe their noses Chateau Charles and his mates have lifted them off and away they go. Christ . . . it's happened to me and hundreds of other lads in the city. A lot of them spend the rest of their lives screwing around cottages and that's sex and that's life and it's their passport round the cities of the world.

And there's money to be made. If you were short of cash and only knew one trade, wouldn't you pull someone off for £50? Aye . . . you can get that sort of money if you know the game well enough.

I've been around . . . got to satisfy your curiosity. You hear the other lads talking about Earls Court and Le Foyer Club, the A and B Club, Rod's in the King's Road . . . that's class . . . and Marc Fleming on a Tuesday night at the Black Cap in Camden Town and you think that's the world and you've got to be part of it for a while so you can tell the others you've made the trip. So I went down to London a couple of summers ago . . . stayed with this man in Highgate, didn't I . . . been writing to him before I met him . . . got his address from this gay mag. He'd made out he lived in a great mansion and had all this money . . . and there was I sixteen years old and what did I know? But when I got there it wasn't like that at all. He just lived with his grandmother and we shared a room and I didn't fancy him at all. He was good to me in a way and took me around for a while. He had a great camera and took pictures that made me look like a model or something . . . but I knew all along that he really wanted to screw me and I didn't want him that way. A year earlier I'd have let him because that's what I used to think it was all about . . . but I'd learnt better and knew that what I wanted mattered as well.

I was in Highgate for about six weeks until his grandmother kicked me out of the flat . . . just locked me out. I came home one day and found my bag on the doorstep and they wouldn't even let me in. So I had nowhere to go and I was really sick . . . so I went to Piccadilly Circus to look for punters and stood outside this cinema in the pouring rain . . . a butch lesbian film, it was . . . and waited to be eyed up . . . which I was . . . but whenever anyone came up to me I panicked and ignored them . . . crazy 'cause I'd done it dozens of times before at home, but London isn't Edinburgh and I hadn't a clue what I was doing down there. They came up an said, 'Are you on?' and I'd ignore them . . . or . . . 'Got a bed for the night?' . . . and I'd walk away and it was still bloody raining and I was getting soaked so I decided to pick a man for myself and I saw this guy and reckoned he was a punter and that he had money and that he wasn't Jack the Ripper and went up to him and said, 'What are you looking for?' And he was bloody foreign, wasn't he, and hardly spoke a word of English but managed to stutter something about where was Trafalgar Square . . . so Christ I told him and wondered whether I would die of pneumonia with the rain soaking me through and I thought Christ what am I going to do?

So I went to Piccadilly Tube Station and went down into it and it was huge and packed with people. And I went to the gents and tried to clean myself up and dry myself and there were other lads there but I was on their territory and they wouldn't have anything to do with me. Then I had a great idea . . . find a phone and ring someone up . . . crazy because I didn't really know anyone but I'd met this guy at a party the week before and if only I could find him in the directory he might help me because I'd gone right off the idea of renting myself by then.

There's loads of phones down there and what with the noise and the people it's difficult to find what you're looking for or hear anything when someone answers at the other end. Anyway I'd just found this number and this man dies . . . just collapses and dies at my feet in the booth next to me . . . just a young guy about twenty and he died right there at my feet . . . it was Heroin or some such drug and he lay there and no one stopped and there were all these hundreds of people and they just ignored him and walked past and over him and I was scared and thank God I got through to the guy I'd met at the party and he told me to get out and get a taxi and come over to his place and he'd pay for it when I arrived and I was in tears when I arrived and couldn't hardly speak and tell him what it had all been like. God . . . now I'm back home and I've given up trolling round the cottages . . . I'm into bars and the contacts I've made for my punters. I've graduated. And that deputy headmaster was nothing exceptional. A load of my custom is teachers and social workers, solicitors, clergymen and I've had policemen on and off duty. You see a lot of them are playing the same game only their rules are slightly different. A lot of the money they get for upholding law and order in Edinburgh goes on rent, doesn't it . . . and it makes me laugh and it makes me bitter and I make them pay for it and that's what my life is. Christ . . . it's the real education they don't teach at school . . . I know there's more truth in the streets of this city than in all the classrooms put end to end.

Philosophy starts with a walk down Princes Street with your eyes open. Take your own trip round the city and see the people, the shops, the *real* traffic, the castle, the parks, the rock, and the trains and ask who for God's sake is really living here.

And we try to brighten our lives with clothes and bars and soul to move our bodies . . . and God . . . SMG discos . . . and Jesus the Traverse Bar and the Palmerstone on a Sunday night and I'm sick . . . sick of it all . . . and I cannot break out and it's the weed that's throttling me, so we laugh and dress up and go searching the Commonwealth Baths for fresh talent that hasn't become neutered with cynicism . . . beautiful young boys that leap at you with a child's joy . . . who can remind you what you were and what you've lost. And that fucking deputy headmaster gave me crabs last night and I've covered my body with lotion to kill them and I'm going out now to find some bastard to lick my body clean and cleanse me . . .